THE POWER TO SPEAK

· REBECCA S. CHOPP ·

THE POWER TO SPEAK

FEMINISM, LANGUAGE, GOD

CROSSROAD · NEW YORK

1989

The Crossroad Publishing Company
370 Lexington Avenue, New York, N.Y. 10017

Printed in the United States of America

Library of Congress Cataloging-in-Publication Data

Chopp, Rebecca S., 1952–
The power to speak : feminism, language, God / Rebecca S. Chopp.
p. cm.
Bibliography: p.
Includes index.
ISBN 0-8245-0940-4
1. Feminist theology. 2. Word of God (Theology) 3. Nonsexist language—Religious aspects—Christianity. I. Title.
BT83.55.C48 1989 89-33953
230'.082—dc20 CIP

Grateful acknowledgment is made to Alfred A. Knopf, Inc., and Wallace Literary Agency for permission to reprint "For Strong Women," from *The Moon Is Always Female* by Marge Piercy. Copyright © 1977, 1979, 1980 by Middlemarsh, Inc.

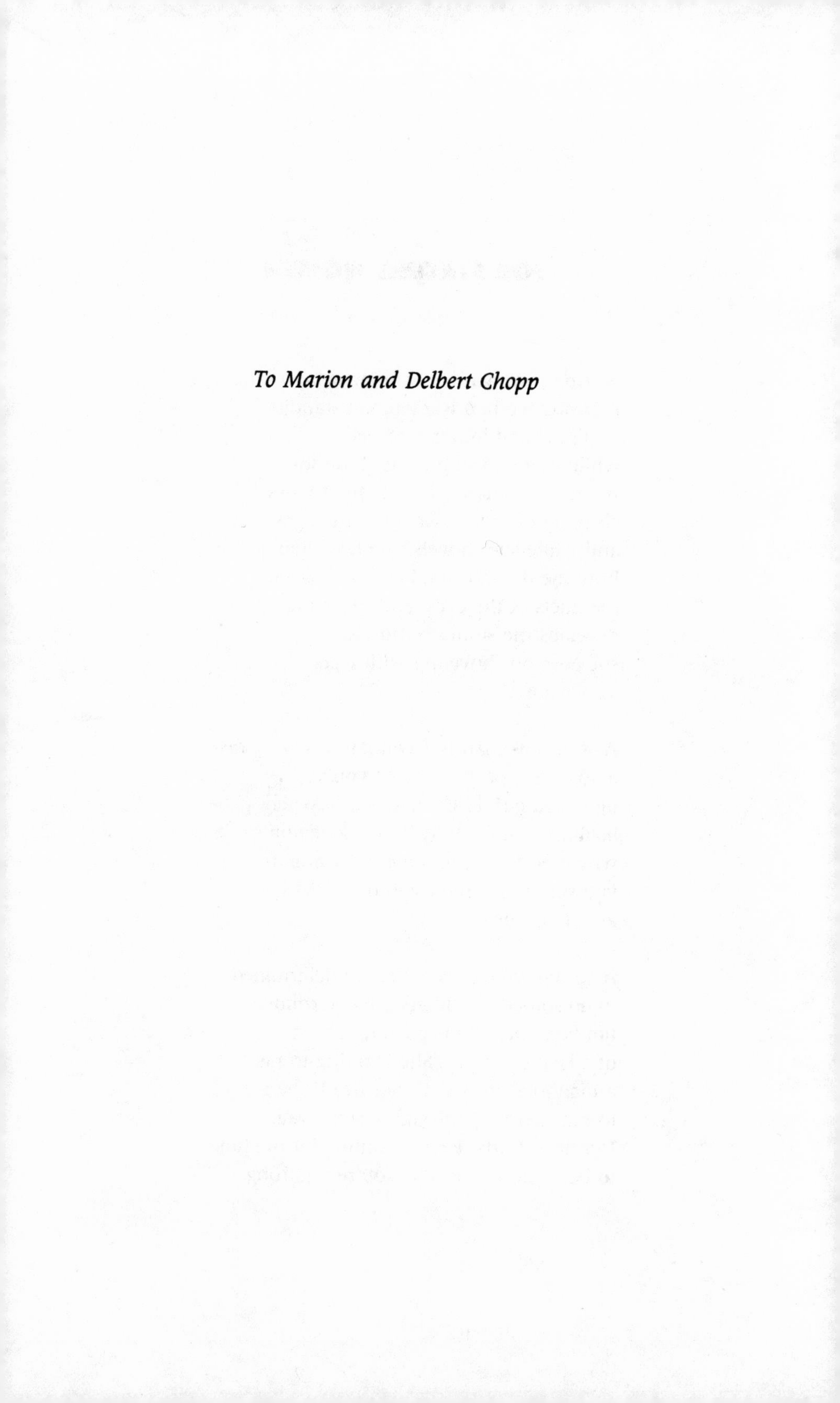

To Marion and Delbert Chopp

FOR STRONG WOMEN

A strong woman is a woman who is straining.
A strong woman is a woman standing
on tiptoe and lifting a barbell
while trying to sing Boris Godunov.
A strong woman is a woman at work
cleaning out the cesspool of the ages,
and while she shovels, she talks about
how she doesn't mind crying, it opens
the ducts of the eyes, and throwing up
develops the stomach muscles, and
she goes on shoveling with tears
in her nose.

A strong woman is a woman in whose head
a voice is repeating, I told you so,
ugly, bad girl, bitch, nag, shrill, witch,
ballbuster, nobody will ever love you back,
why aren't you feminine, why aren't
you soft, why aren't you quiet, why
aren't you dead?

A strong woman is a woman determined
to do something others are determined
not be done. She is pushing up on the bottom
of a lead coffin lid. She is trying to raise
a manhole cover with her head, she is trying
to butt her way through a steel wall.
Her head hurts. People waiting for the hole
to be made say, hurry, you're so strong.

A strong woman is a woman bleeding
inside. A strong woman is a woman making
herself strong every morning while her teeth
loosen and her back throbs. Every baby,
a tooth, midwives used to say, and now
every battle a scar. A strong woman
is a mass of scar tissue that aches
when it rains and wounds that bleed
when you bump them and memories that get up
in the night and pace in boots to and fro.

A strong woman is a woman who craves love
like oxygen or she turns blue choking.
A strong woman is a woman who loves
strongly and weeps strongly and is strongly
terrified and has strong needs. A strong woman is strong
in words, in action, in connection, in feeling;
she is not strong as a stone but as a wolf
suckling her young. Strength is not in her, but she
enacts it as the wind fills a sail.

What comforts her is others loving
her equally for the strength and for the weakness
from which it issues, lightning from a cloud.
Lightning stuns. In rain, the clouds disperse.
Only water of connection remains,
flowing through us. Strong is what we make
each other. Until we are all strong together,
a strong woman is a woman strongly afraid.

Marge Piercy

CONTENTS

ACKNOWLEDGMENTS

This book seeks to encourage words about Word and to envision Word for and with words. Yet it is hard to find words appropriate to express my gratitude to all those who have traveled with me in this logological and theological journey. Joe Columbo, Roberta Bondi, Heindrikus Boers, Carol Newsom, David Pacini, William Mallard, Charles Gerkin, Jim Fowler, David Tracy, Walt Lowe, Rod Hunter, Ken Langston, and Jamie Scott have given me support, comments, corrections, and ideas. With brilliance and calmness, Justus George Lawler has given me understanding, suggestions, encouragement, and most of all, was willing to transform free-flowing insights into theological discourse. Numerous institutions, institutes, groups, and churches have heard parts of this text, and I have profited greatly from conversations in these places. More than any other institution, I am indebted to my own, Candler School of Theology, Emory University, for supporting me during the writing of this book. Dean Jim Waits deserves special mention, not only for granting me house leave to work on this manuscript, but for his own tremendous personal enthusiasm for and interest in systematic theology.

Millie Feske, Alicia Frank, and Pam Johnson have "heard me into speech" about this book in many ways. Bettie Banks, Kathleen Waller, Barbara Wheeler, Inagrace Dietterich, Kathy Yeager—strong women all of them—interlace across my life, providing vision and joy. I want to acknowledge with deep appreciation two friends who always welcome me amid all the pleasures and pains life offers: Susan Shapiro, a close friend of many years whose work influences mine greatly, seemed always available to consider the argument of this text and to discover and create new strategies and approaches; and Eliza Ellison, who literally saw me write and rewrite this text, who read and reread the drafts, and who kept me inspired with wonderful women's literature. The steadfastness of both of these friends has given me the power to speak many times over.

Words fall short when it comes to thanking those whose support is nearly endless. Mark Biddle, my husband, has always provided endless encouragement for my writing. Nate Biddle, my son, has helped in many ways. Finally, I must thank my parents, Marion and Delbert Chopp, to whom this book is dedicated, for sharing with me the many blessings of life, and encouraging in my life creativity, determination, and independence of thought.

INTRODUCTION

Since "God" by definition transcends all symbol-systems, we must begin, like theology, by noting that language is intrinsically unfitted to discuss the "supernatural" literally. For language is empirically confined to terms referring to physical nature, terms referring to socio-political relationships and terms describing language itself. Hence, all the words for "God" must be used analogically—as were we to speak of God's "powerful arm" (a physical analogy), or of God as "lord" or "father" (a socio-political analogy) or of God as the "Word" (a linguistic analogy).

Kenneth Burke

I want to posit the possibility that there is a word, that there are many words, awaiting woman speech. And perhaps there is a word that has not yet come to sound—a word that once we begin to speak will round out and create deeper experiences for us and put us in touch with sources of power, energy of which we are just beginning to be aware.

Nelle Morton

I have, I think, few romantic illusions concerning "woman" as a collective singular, but I probably have even fewer illusions about women in all their differences and specificity simply fitting into the present social-symbolic order, modern Christianity, and contemporary theology.[1] As Helene Cixous points out, the principle ordering gender relations in politics and subjectivity—the place of men and women, the experience of men and women—is exemplified by, and in turn governs from, its centrality in language. It is exemplified by

> dual, *hierarchized* oppositions. Superior/inferior. Myths, legends, books. Philosophical systems. Wherever an ordering intervenes, a law

> organizes thè thinkable by (dual, irreconcilable; or mitigable, dialectical) oppositions. And all the couples of oppositions are *couples.* Does this mean something? Is the fact that logocentrism subjects thought—all of the concepts, the codes, the values—to a two-term system, related to "the" couple man/woman?[2]

The basic patterning, organizing, ordering principle of thought and language, and thus that of the social and symbolic order as the dominant practices and principles in language, subjectivity, and politics, is the opposition of two terms, an opposition that forces and reinforces the basic couple of man/woman.

Against this social-symbolic organization where, as Deborah Cameron has observed, "men can be men only if women are unambiguously women," women must develop new discourses for their lives, writing and speaking their stories not through the closure of an eternal division between man and woman, but through adventure, laughter, openness, freedom, creativity, and friendship.[3] Carolyn Heilbrun, in *Writing a Woman's Life,* argues that in order to develop new discourses women must exercise their power, especially the power to create the stories of one's own becoming. Heilbrun puts it this way: "Power is the ability to take one's place in whatever discourse is essential to action and the right to have one's part matter."[4] If, as Heilbrun insists, women must have the power to write their lives, so also must women have the power to speak: to speak of their multiplicity and differences, their pleasures and their tribulations, their longings and their comforts.

Women, however, are bound to be strangers forever unless new ways of speaking can give voice to what it has been to be the female term—not only the times of pain, but also the spaces of pleasure it has created. Women will be forever strangers unless their words and their voices revise the social and symbolic rules of language, transforming the law of ordered hierarchy in language, in subjectivity, and in politics into a grace of rich plenitude for human flourishing. With Cixous and other women theorists and women poets, women must find ways of resisting the codes, the concepts, the values, and the structures that are subject to this two-term system. In this fashion women may not so much balance or equalize the hierarchy as change its monotheistic ordering of the "one" as opposed to the "other" into a multiplicity, allowing differences and connections instead of constantly guaranteeing identities and oppositions.[5]

This is not a book on language and politics, though it considers both in the proclamation of emancipatory transformation. Rather it is a book on language as a political activity.[6] The interpretive reading of this book presupposes a need to change prevailing discourses, to multiply possible signifiers, and to enrich the signifying process; to create and discover new discourses of what it is to be human, what it is to be free, what it is to live together. Therefore, this text challenges many of the reigning discourses, especially those having to do with subjectivity, politics, language, community, textuality, God, and women. At least in the judgment of this writer, feminism must nudge the reigning discourses long enough to raise questions about the practices and terms in and of our language and to excite the aesthetic imaging of new symbols, terms, significations, and practices.

Precisely as a work in language is a political activity for feminists, this is a theological work, seeking to uncover the theological, linguistic, and political ordering that has so long, throughout various manifestations of patriarchy, opposed women to the Word, and so denied women access to speaking of words and Word.[7] Theology is knowledge and words about God, and linguistically, God is understood as the Word. As Word, God has traditionally been prevented from being represented by woman, while woman has been configured as taboo and placed on the margins of the Word. Yet there is a curious phenomenon occurring today in that women, from the margins of the social, political, linguistic, and theological order, do speak of the Word, and speak to proclaim this Word to and for the world. Both the ways and substance of women speaking, expressed in various feminist theologies, encourage the possibilities for speaking and acting as proclamations of the Word.

This book seeks to examine and construct feminist theology as discourses of emancipatory transformation that proclaim the Word to and for the world. It is an interpretation of feminist theology and a reconstruction of proclamation and the Word in Christian theology.[8] In this manner, the book tries to express the good news of feminist theology which is, today, the good news for and of Christianity.

An analogy may be helpful to identify the interpretation of feminist theology as a reconstruction of a theology of proclamation. Karl Rahner bequeathed to us the notion that the church is the sacrament of God in the world.[9] Utilizing this insight, many liberation theologians have not only given rich new meaning to the sacraments, but have also provided a new purpose and vitality to the church.[10] In fundamental agreement with the church as the sacrament of God's grace in the world, this book seeks to make a related claim about the church's proclamation as discourses of emancipatory transformation for the world.

Proclamation, too long limited (like the sacraments) to intra-ecclesiological confines, now must be articulated through the church for the world. As proclamation leaves its ecclesial prison, speaking now of Word for and with world, so it loosens its confinement in the preached word, becoming now the fullness of discourse: the images, stories, voices, symbols, interpretations, and aesthetic productions that Christianity offers in solidarity with a world so desperately seeking to speak of freedom in new ways. The church, then, proclaims God in the world by offering discourses of emancipatory transformation. Furthermore, the church makes such discourses persuasive, by embodying and expressing the fluidity of images, texts, voices, and figures of freedom that it creates and discovers in the words that give rise to person's lives, in the words that speak of freedom in the Book, in the words of praise and communion in the community, in the words enlivened by the Word.

The church has formed its proclamation to the world in various ways, discovering in the lively intersection of the Scriptures and Christian piety, discourses that speak to the needs and desires of the world. In former days when church and empire were intimately interwoven this was clearly the case, yet in modern times there have been instances in which Christianity has spoken powerfully for those both in and out of the church.[11] Reinhold Niebuhr, whose works to this day help many name the delicate balances of power, the struggles of pride, and the reality of sin, is but one recent example.[12] The theological reconstruction involved in this book relies on the assumption that the formation of Christian discourse is, in fact, not only appropriate to but, in fact, called for in much of the tradition; indeed, the present theological reconstruction seeks to provoke and encourage the revision of Christian witness in the present day. Because of this judgment, this work moves away from configuring itself within present theological debates of methodological norms and procedures, preferring, instead, to explore possibilities for speaking a living Word to and for the world.

As Rahner's insight arises from the Catholic experience of church and sacrament, so this one stems from the Protestant experience of church and Word, but, in a fashion similar to Rahner's insight, for the whole of Christianity. It is a retrieval of the Protestant insistence on the living, dynamic communication between God and world.[13] Though proclamation theologies are often said to begin in the unbridgeable gap between God and world, my understanding of proclamation and the Word as a way of speaking of God and world argues for a relationship between gap and connection, relying, in a manner somewhat similar to Paul Tillich's, on the manifestation of both abyss and source.[14] Language itself, after all, depends upon a certain intersubjectivity, an interconnectedness that bridges gaps—else why would we need speech? Yet language is utterly dependent upon the gap, abyss, and separation that require communication. This, we can assume, is one of the reasons that the Word has been spoken of as sacramental, a visible sign of God's invisible grace, because the living Word is present in words as the fullness, the connection, as well as the abyss of all words.[15]

Though this book itself will not inquire into the history of theologies of proclamation, it may be helpful to sort out the present relationship of Protestantism and the Word. Historically, Protestant theologies placed the Word at the center of their reflection, understanding theology's purpose to relate God's Word to the world. But contemporary Protestant theology contains hardly any reflection on the theological status of proclamation or of the Word, an absence which perhaps contributes to the general malaise in Protestant theology or to what Jürgen Moltmann has called the dual crisis of identity and relevance.[16] If Protestant theology has any identity to find or, more to my interests, if Protestant theology has anything to contribute to Christian theology and Christianity in general, such a contribution requires a reconsideration of proclamation and the Word. Is the identity of Protestant theology and Protestant Christianity now secured only through institutional affiliation, or is there some meaning in the Reformation insistence that God is revealed, experienced, and present in the proclaimed Word?

Protestant theology, at least as defined by modern revisionist schools, both liberal and neoorthodox, worries over its own lack of relevance today.[17] Part of this lack is that its message, that is, the Word in, with, and to the world, has lost its power of interpretation and transformation. The proclaimed Word is understood, occasionally, as no more than comfort for the weak in times of despair, or, more frequently, as incapable of addressing the fundamental questions that are central for the Christian community and for human existence. Does Christianity have anything to say to the present world situation? Does the Word live through the church's words proclaiming grace, love, freedom, redemption, and hope in a world that is struggling in the chaos of evil and sin?

Protestant theology's last great interpretation of the Word remains the theologies of Karl Barth and Rudolph Bultmann and the revision of these theologies in the works of Gerhard Ebeling and Ernst Fuchs.[18] These neoorthodox options present problems for today's theological reflection. First of all, many of the neoorthodox theologies of proclamation represent the Word of God as *channeled through* human words, the event character of the Word receiving no content or influence by human words or experience. This is philosophically suspect, since recent hermeneutical philosophy refuses to separate the message from the myth in a way that these theologians found so easy. It is also philosophically problematic since many of the neoorthodox theologians understood the event character of the Word to be primarily existential, appealing to the individual consciousness while contemporary philosophers of language place increased emphasis on the communal character of language and the linguistic constitution of community. This philosophical problem has an experiential parallel in the increased commitment in contemporary Christian witness to the reality of *community* as the primary referent for religious experience. Many contemporary Christians desire a Christian faith constituted not through belief structures based on a particular idea of God or through the piety of an individual relationship to Christ but in belonging to Christian communities marked by both pluralism and ambiguity within which they carry out their discipleship to the world. Indeed it might well be argued that neoorthodoxy ignored, despite its own desires, the Christian affirmation of the Word as always a Word of relationship, communion, and communication that, in the context of community, is always constituted through and in communicative solidarity with human words, relations, and actions.[19]

This brings me to one final observation before outlining the flow of this book. My discourse attempts, in its own strategies, to criticize and move toward transforming the social-symbolic order. I do not think that women can opt out of this order to make up new discourses, nor do I think correcting the order is enough. Even as a strategy for promoting feminism, separation neglects the need to transform the order not only for ourselves, but for others: for the dead and those who have suffered, the living who do not yet speak, and those not yet born who will have voices to speak. But I do think transformation is necessary; for modern linguistic practices and discourses, which reflect and contribute to subjectivity and politics, do not allow for otherness, specificity, difference, solidarity, and transformation.[20] Until we change the values and hidden rules that run through present linguistic practices, social codes, and psychic orderings, women, persons of color, and other oppressed groups will be forced—by the language, discourses, and practices available to them—into conforming to ongoing practices, to babbling nonsense, or to not speaking at all. Such transformation is how I understand the movement of feminist theology. To name it explicitly, in the manner I have done, is to hurry us on the way where women may speak and hear in their differences, in their specificity, in their connections, and in their solidarity with the world.

I begin, in the first chapter, by interpreting feminist theologies, concentrating on several recent works, as discourses of emancipatory transformation that proclaim the Word to and for the world. Such discourses are the production of Christian witness in the contemporary situation, a witness that makes the good news known through emancipatory transformation in terms of difference, specificity, embodiment, solidarity, anticipation, and transformation.[21] Understanding feminist theologies as discourses of emancipatory transformation that *are* proclamations allows us to attend to the process and substance of reading the Scriptures, forming community, and speaking to the world in feminist theology.

Yet the linguistic and theological naming of feminist discourses must move with great care in terms of its theological warrants: addressing the conditions of possibility for its own discourse by considering the relation between women and the Word. Despite the influx of women into leadership roles in the church and teaching roles in the academy, I am not sure that women's "otherness" is either heard or spoken. Is solving the problems in theological speaking and listening only a matter of prophetic injunction and polite intent to let the "other" in? Or is a more fundamental change required, a revisioning of how we speak, a reordering of theological discourse that permits multiplicity, difference, and creativity instead of protecting identity, definition, and explanation? Moving to a reconsideration of the relation between women and the Word, a relationship which has formed the Word as primal referent and women as taboo, this chapter reconstructs in a theological semiotics the proclaimed Word as the perfectly open sign that funds multiplicity and otherness in and through feminist discourses. The reconstruction of the Word then empowers the construction of feminist discourses in a theological pragmatics through the logic of abduction or dynamic transformation, the play of aesthetics, and the practices of rhetoric.[22] To some, these questions may seem unnecessarily abstract, though it is necessary to recognize that anonymous rules and hidden principles, which may be unveiled best through abstraction, are, in often unacknowledged ways, the most practical realities of all.

The second chapter considers proclamation in relation to the Scriptures, but it does so quite concretely through a reading of Luke 4:16–30, appropriately a proclamation narrative. This chapter faces, as does the text as a whole, the difficult task of at one and the same time trying to provoke a new way of doing things and trying to illustrate the substance of this new way. The hermeneutical understanding employed in this chapter opposes the modern way of reading for one meaning, a meaning that mirrors the intentions of a self. Instead a more "restless" hermeneutics is employed, one that, with much recent hermeneutical theory, attempts to engage the reader in a dialogue, a dialogue that respects the historicity of both reader and text. This chapter relies on two theological judgments in feminist theology: the first, that of Elisabeth Schüssler Fiorenza, on understanding the Bible through the notion of prototype and not archetype, and the second, a hermeneutics of marginality that reads the Scriptures in term of their credible claims to freedom.[23] Rather than speaking only about hermeneutical principles, I have chosen to employ hermeneutical principles to read a text. In this manner I hope to receive from the text as much as I can for a vision of emancipatory proclamation (as shall be seen, however, my attempt is somewhat undercut or decentered, if not displaced, by the text itself).

If proclamation occurs in and through the Word and in dialogue with Scriptures, as discussed in chapter 2, it also occurs in the church, and this occurrence is the topic of chapter 3. The theological turn I argue for envisions the purpose and nature of the church as a community constituted through and for its proclamation to the world. Such a revisioning of the church, a reconstructed logic of the *ecclesia,* is an exceedingly difficult task, since despite the desires for community in modern theology, it is quite clear that conditions for any substantive sense of community are far from us. In this text, women-church (by which I mean the movement of women in, partially in, and utterly outside the institutional church) provides the basis for beginning to describe a community that lives in and for the proclamation of God in the world. But I use women-church in relation to the terms set for the church as community by Friedrich Schleiermacher and Karl Barth, for the ambiguities of their discourse provide the sources for a feminist transformation. Despite their focus on the relation between God and the individual both of these theologians maintain a desire to place community as central to the continuity or receptivity of Christianity.[24] To me one of the most hopeful signs in the middle-class church is the desire of many—including its theologians—for community, and this desire, coupled with the reality and the vision of women-church provides a new way to speak of a Christian community that is formed in and through the Word but always and only to and for the world.

Speaking to and for the world is the general theme of my last chapter, but it is a theme which needs (as does chapter 2 on the Scriptures) the actual production (or at least the selection of resources for production) at least as much as it needs the fine tunings of analytical procedures. Thus I begin the chapter with a quick draft of a grand theory, an interpretive analytics of what Christian witness should be speaking against in the social-symbolic order, which, predictably, focuses on the ordering principles in language, subjectivity, and politics. Feminist theology can offer resources for a proclamation of emancipatory transformation to a situation in which narcissistic individualism, representational language, and the politics of self-preservation prevent human flourishing. But along the way I make clear my understanding of feminist theology in the present scene, before I begin my own play of images, readings, terms, and relations out of women's experience in the margins of the social-symbolic order.

This book is but an opening in conversation, an attempt to cast and configure what we might need if we were, in Christianity and theology, to take seriously language as a site of transformation in subjectivity and politics. The medium of theology, after all, is words, and words about God as well as words about words need careful attention in the present era. The text arises out of women's ability and frustration in speaking, not only out of the pain of oppression but also out of the visions of flourishing that seep from the margins and fissures in the present situation. Clearly, it is not itself yet a satisfactory proclamation of emancipatory transformation, though it is, at least in desire, part of what must be signified, dreamed, and spoken as Christianity, including Christian theology, speaks again the Word to and with the world.

·1·

PROCLAMATION, WOMEN, AND THE WORD

The honey-mad woman offers herself as totem, as ancestress, as an explorer who gives us a map for defining a countertradition within women's writing, a tradition in which the woman writer appropriates the language "racked up" in her own body and starts to sing. A blissful consumer and purveyor of language, the honey-mad writer is a symbol of verbal plenitude, of woman's capacity to rewrite her culture.

Patricia Yaeger

To Speak of Freedom

How do we speak of freedom in a world of suffering? Must we not voice the desire of freedom in the voices of those who have been murdered? What is it to be free in a world exploding between the rich and the poor? Do words of freedom make any sense when the horizon of history is that of apocalyptic doom? Can the middle class be free from their suicidal conformity to individualism and consumerism?[1] Is freedom primarily personal or communal? We must speak of freedom, and it is the hardest of all words to speak. That we (and I mean by this a worldly we) must speak of freedom only indicates very broadly the quest and questions in the present situation. To speak of freedom is no longer an empty, formal claim about a general philosophy of history, but a brimming, material claim about the very desire of our lives. This desire, the desire of speaking of freedom, is a particular and "concrete" activity, voicing and governing suffering, unrest, subversiveness, laughter, desire, hope, and pleasure. To speak of freedom names, at least in some fashion, both the need and the desire of most of the people around the world.

The phrase "to speak of freedom" is decidedly tensive, functioning to describe the risks of freedom as well as the ambiguities of freedom. It is a way of holding together in fragility and power the voices and bodies of the oppressed as they speak. To speak of freedom by those who have not represented the universal human subject is not only to dare to grasp one's own subjectivity but also, in this very risky act, to acknowledge the pleasure and pain of who one already is. This act of affirmation against all the forces of denial is also an act of survival, for if we do not find ways to speak of freedom and its promise—for the future, for all together, for babies, and for those who suffer—then we speak of freedom for no one. But this phrase, "to speak of freedom," also calls to mind the modern history of the autonomous subject and its claims for freedom in the midst of the horrors of modern civilization's holocausts, nuclear threats, and economic disasters.[2] To speak of freedom is thus a way, at least, to speak amid the ambiguities and margins of modern discourse, and in this speaking to move beyond this discourse even as the modern vision passes beyond its own methods and models.[3]

To speak of freedom, now, means more than interrupting current discourse and practices; it demands more than simply saying no to the terrors of modernity. Ways must be found not only to describe the chains of words and practices that imprison, but also to name the possibilities and dreams of freedom as emancipation and transformation.[4] In such a manner, the discourses of feminist theologies, like the discourses of liberation theologies in general, are not simply discourses about the limitations and oppressiveness of modern Christianity, but discourses of different ways of being and doing; they are not merely discourses aimed at gaining admittance for their speakers into the system, they are discourses intent on transforming the system with visions of new ways of being human.[5] What the variety of discourses of feminist theologies share in common is the desire to speak of freedom, to envision new ways of being human, to speak of the desires of women, and to speak of what women have known, what have been women's burdens, and what woman has experienced as the "other" of man. This is not to imply that feminist theologians are all in basic agreement in regard to the nature, forms, and tasks of feminist theology, or even in regard to strategies of linguistic usage.[6] Indeed, feminist theologians formulate their discourses for distinct purposes: from Mary Daly's playful rebirthing of words to create women's space, to Sallie McFague's careful working within the metaphorical constructs of present theological language to demand their flexibility, to Elisabeth Schüssler Fiorenza's creative blending of historical scholarship and women's poetry to form new methods of biblical interpretation, to Rosemary Radford Ruether's alternating use of the methods of prosaic imaging and modern analytics to move us toward a feminist theology.[7] All of these forms are important and, I want to contend, integral to feminist theology, for feminist theologians proclaim, in a variety of ways, the importance of speaking and hearing the otherness and the multiplicity of women, and, for most feminist theologians, the otherness and multiplicity of all oppressed groups. Thus, feminist theology is an activity of and in language and discourse, an activity that enables the privileging of multiplicity and difference even in our speaking and hearing.

Such a requirement, I want to suggest, necessitates attention to the nature of language (how language works) and discourse (the historical forms of our language).[8] Such attention not only enriches the vitality of feminist theology as composed of a multiplicity of discourses, allowing otherness, difference, and solidarity to occur in and through this multiplicity, but also brings forth the religious vitality of these discourses. Feminist theology expresses deep religious sensitivity, words full of Word, and, as such, words of grace, healing, wholeness, new possibilities, and crucifixion and resurrection. To understand how feminist discourses proclaim Word to and for the world is to speak of God, and of God's movement in the margins and fissures of the world.

Recent trends in contemporary theory have focused on language as a way to move out of the foundationalism of the past, as a way to deal with the historicity and creativity of human culture, and as a way to criticize and transform, in some related fashion, the figures, terms, and principles that subjectivity, politics, and language share in the present historical period.[9] Language serves as both the material and the frame for structural and cultural debates about the role of women, affirmative action, and issues such as birth control, abortion, and child care. Yet language is also the site where our subjectivity is formed; we think and feel, we experience the world according to the categories given to us by language. What it is to be a woman or a man varies in different cultures and at different times and places, but these definitions are prior to the individual, indeed, they allow the individual to become man or woman in the acceptable modes of that culture.

Simone de Beauvoir remarked, "One is not born a woman, one becomes a woman."[10] One becomes a woman by wearing pink and lace in infancy, by receiving presents of dolls, by being complimented for neatness and niceness, by finding one's happiness in parties and clothes, by speaking a language where the feminine is inferior and different from the masculine. What it is to be a woman is constituted by discourses about sexual gender, such as the traditional discourses of the cult of the domestic woman or the Virgin Mary or the contemporary discourse displayed in current women's magazines of the superwoman who holds both a full-time professional job and a full-time job as wife and mother. Though often differing as to the forms of meaning they construct, these discourses create forms of subjectivity for women in ways that are historically specific.[11] By becoming a woman through these social codes, these rules of discourse, these cultural practices, the gaining of subjectivity occurs simultaneously with the guaranteeing of the social-symbolic order. Such discourses can change, be displaced, or be transformed and the change of discourse allows different forms of subjectivity to appear. Feminist consciousness raising, for instance, occurs when women discover that their frustrations, inner turmoils, and unmet desires are due not to their individual failure to measure up or be good enough but to social structures that devalue women and limit their opportunities for fulfillment. Consciousness raising works, it can be said, by introducing a new discourse that transforms the meaning of women's experience.[12]

Language is also the site of politics, since discourses form various political options, structures, and procedures. Indeed, since language does not originate in the intentions of the speakers, politics, in a most basic sense, is the social contract of meanings at a particular time to which individuals are subject.[13] For instance, consider the two most popular discourses of dealing with criminal offenders: a discourse of punishment requires structures to narrow the limits of freedom and pleasure for the wrongdoer; while a discourse of rehabilitation seeks to broaden opportunities for the socially and/or psychologically disadvantaged. American presidential politics, to take another example, is (ideally) a choice among competing discourses, and voters are forced to select, by opting for one candidate, the discourse that defines which issues are important, how these issues will be addressed, and how the meaning and practices of the United States will be officially represented and administered.

Language bridges the gap between individual subjectivity, cultural practices, and societal institutions, providing a way to cross the mysterious waters of the norms, values, and principles that operate in various dimensions, places, and ways throughout the social-symbolic order. For instance, the rule of individuality operates in modern subjectivity, wherein the "I" is seen as a fixed identity expressing the self in history; in modern practices of reading and writing, which focus on the individual intent of author, text, or reader; in modern politics, which supposedly is composed of individuals cooperating together for a common good which persons as individuals agree upon; and in modern theology, which secures God through individual consciousness or receptivity.

The phrase "social-symbolic order" calls attention, in linguistic fashion, to how a dominant ordering operates in subjectivity, language, and politics. The social-symbolic order might also be called the present historical situation or contemporary existence. But the phrase "the social-symbolic order" underscores the structural as well as the symbolic perspectives of language.[14] This ordering is an economy, a patterning of certain values and principles establishing often anonymous rules that run through discourses about different arenas and different discourses about one arena of social life. The qualifier social-symbolic indicates that this ordering, though dominant in a particular historical period or era, is nonetheless a historical construct, and thus open to change and transformation.

Language, at least as it is used in feminist discourse, involves a creativity, a fluidity, or what Hannah Arendt called a natality.[15] Language, according to the usage employed in this book, can birth new meanings, new discourses, new signifying practices. Deborah Cameron has suggested that such an integrationalist approach acknowledges that language cannot be separated from other social institutions, nor abstracted from time and space, and must be respected as a creative process.[16] Though there is a social-symbolic order, an ordering of language, subjectivity, and politics, such ordering is not totalitarian in the day-to-day life of society. Around the social-symbolic order are margins and fissures that allow language and thus the social-symbolic order to be corrected, changed, subverted, interrupted, and transformed.

Such a focus on language calls forth a new interpretation of the nature and function of feminist theologies. Feminist theologies exist in the crisis of modernity, the crisis of transforming a social-symbolic order that has been dominated by terms of identity, autonomy, representationality, self-preservation, and presence. As Zillah Eisenstein has argued, though feminism emerged from the theories and practices of liberalism concerning individual autonomy, it has to undermine liberalism's foundation both in terms of the hidden principles of autonomy and individuality, and in terms of the institutionalization of the separation between the public and private realms.[17] Feminism, including feminist theology, has become a critique and transformation of not only modernity's figuration and construction of woman, but also the rules and principles of modernity that weave through its practices of politics, subjectivity, reading, speaking, culture, and language.

Marginality and Emancipatory Transformation: The Positioning of Feminist Discourse

No one can stand on all the margins of the social-symbolic order at once, indeed the need to speak of freedom is today the need to speak of it in one's own specificity and difference and from this place to envision connection to and solidarity with others. I stand in the margins of feminist discourse and from this position of marginality to the social-symbolic order I speak. By marginal I do not mean trivial or unnecessary, though that is the way that women and feminism have often been cast. (Women, as feminists have often pointed out, are essential to the maintenance of society, our bodies the precondition to culture.) Rather, the language of marginality suggests the systemic devaluing of women wherein women are valued less than men; women are, in one sense of the word, more "marginal," meaning they are less than, they do not have as much importance. But marginal also means the effacing of women, for women are not men, and hence are not really present and can be overlooked: in this sense marginal means having no substance, containing nothing, the emptiness of the margins. Marginal implies also the notion of borderline or limit or edge, as a margin defines the edges of a text. Here women are cast as the border—literally, the margin—which demarcates order and chaos. As the border of the social-symbolic order women take on characteristics of the chaos so feared by the order, but as outer rim of the order, women can take on characteristics revered by the order. Toril Moi portrays the working of marginality in this manner:

> Women seen as the limit of the symbolic order will in other words share in the disconcerting properties of *all* frontiers: they will be neither inside nor outside, neither known or unknown. It is this position that has enabled male culture sometimes to vilify women as representing darkness and chaos, to view them as Lilith or the Whore of Babylon, and sometimes to elevate them as the representatives of a

> higher and purer nature, to venerate them as Virgins and Mothers of God. In this first instance the border line is seen as part of the chaotic wilderness outside, and in the second it is seen as an inherent part of the inside: the part that protects and shields the symbolic order from the imaginary chaos.[18]

In this text, feminism is the discourse of and from this position of marginality. The term "feminism" has carried certain connotations that tend to dilute the radicality of the discourse by suggesting, for instance, that the telos of feminist theology is either to call God "she," thus not touching God at all, or to place women in bureaucracies of the social-symbolic order, thus not disturbing the order at all. Other connotations of the term "feminism" have operated in relation to the selectivity of the term "women's experience" and have reduced the complexity of different women, assuming somehow that women's experience is separable from the social-symbolic order. Despite all these problematic connotations, feminism means speaking from the position of marginality.[19] Feminism is not somehow just about women; rather, it casts its voice from the margins over the whole of the social-symbolic order, questioning its rules, terms, procedures, and practices.

At this point it must be said that, in relation to the images of margin and center, I am an uneasy modern, a member in good standing, yet one who will not dismiss the new discourses of liberation theologies and political theologies. Claiming one's voice on the margins does not make one deaf; rather, it gives new ways to hear, new eyes to see, and new possibilities for solidarity. Between the openness to the voices of liberation and political theologians, and to feminist and womanist voices not my own, I also understand that as a white, middle-class, well-educated woman I am part of the center.[20] The center is, in modernity, cracking, its fissures are widening, and in these fissures and cracks, discourses of emancipatory transformation may be formed. The place of a white middle-class feminist is, on the one hand, forever marginal to the center of the order as related to patriarchal relations and monotheistic ordering, but is also part of the center as related to economic and racial realities. Yet precisely from this center/margin viewpoint, I see that the order works for no one, and thus any discourse of freedom and God from my place has the role of making co-present the suffering of the margins with the psychic destructiveness of the center.[21] This is where I stand, with both blindness and insight, in a place from which I must listen and speak.

It is this same space, at the same time marginal and yet participating in the center, that has given rise to what is called feminist theology. In the beginning, feminist theology functioned as a hermeneutics of suspicion, a corrective to Christian theology "proper," asking questions such as, How had women been excluded from the text? Was women's experience represented in common human experience? Were there texts written by women? This work of systematic questioning revealed that Christianity, despite promises and symbols of radical freedom for all, had systematically ordered itself through a gender division of men and women combined with a hierarchy of God-male-female-nature. But this work, in its initial stages, went on within the confines of modern Christian theology, never questioning modern theology's basic assumptions and rules for discourse.[22]

Yet the questioning of feminist theology became the question of women's power to speak of freedom and soon exceeded any merely corrective enterprise. For in the constant interpretation and uncovering of the patriarchy that has been Christianity, women began to question the basic assumptions and boundaries of Christianity itself. Women began to wonder about the term "common human experience," about a vision of God as utterly beyond or at the limits of human experience, and about the methods as well as the results of biblical scholarship. Feminist theology began not merely to correct but to change, not merely to be suspicious but to proclaim: to proclaim God and freedom, hope and humanity, in new ways and new forms. The language shifted: rather than demanding "let us in," feminists began saying, "share our vision."

But it is precisely at this point that one asks why women stay in Christianity, or alternatively, where is the point or limit when feminist theology is no longer Christian? Is there not, as is often queried, a contradiction between feminism and Christianity? Sometimes feminist theologians have responded to this contradiction by arguing that one simply is Christian and cannot really choose to leave Christianity, or, in other words, that Christianity is their religious home. Such argument, though speaking to the emotional bonds of women to Christianity, disposes critics to reject Christianity as a "burdensome tradition" and to view Christian feminists as adolescents who cannot leave the "home" of Christianity, even when it curtails or impedes their freedom. It too easily determines Christianity as a kind of prison of speech and contradicts the impulses of feminism as, at least minimally, an affirmation of women's ability to question and create. It leads, as well, to a peculiar positioning of some feminist religious discourse as "post-Christian," a maturation beyond the home of Christian tradition.[23]

Instead, I want to suggest that women "stay" in Christianity not because it is a burdensome tradition, a home that one can never leave no matter how far one travels, but because feminist theology reconstructs Christianity into discourses of emancipatory transformation, discourses that, through a multiplicity of strategies, allow each woman to speak her self, her desires, her time and space, her hopes, her God.[24] The radical activity of feminist theology is, in my judgment, nothing short of a portend of a transformation of Christianity itself. Such a transformation can be identified best through examining the discursive practices of feminist theology, and expanding these practices to the transformation of basic Christian loci such as proclamation, Word, Scripture, church, and witness to the world.

Feminist theology, at least in some recent works, can be best construed as discourses from the margins that free women's voices to transform, rather than merely correct, the social-symbolic order. Such a reading does not silence the debates between feminists, but names the shared praxis of feminist theologies by finding ways for women to speak that encourage multiplicity and otherness. That feminist theologies are about emancipatory transformation goes, I assume, without much argument, but what must be recognized is that the discourses of feminist theology engage in emancipatory transformation through the inclusion of multiple strategies, provoking multiple images of human flourishing and images of difference, otherness, solidarity, and transformation. The discourses of feminist theology use a variety of genres and strategies to transform the system. In other words, to redefine the order through the marginality of women, to generate difference, multiplicity, otherness, specificity, transformation, and solidarity in language and discourse is itself an activity of emancipatory transformation.

Through language and discourse, then, emerges emancipatory transformation, an emancipatory transformation that invokes, blesses, and pours out multiplicity and otherness through the constant blending of strategies, genres, terms, and sources. Thus Rosemary Radford Ruether's *Sexism and God-Talk*—in which the major body of the text is ordered through modern theological discourse—blends, almost without hesitation, basic neoorthodox principles of theology and a revised critical correlation method of theology to move (note her limiting term) *toward* a feminist theology.[25] Implicit in this writing is a furthering of modern theological discourse for feminist ends. Thus far, Ruether can be criticized for remaining mortgaged to methods of humanistic theology. But she surrounds her text with two fascinating pieces of prose: the first is a feminist "midrash on the gospel in three acts," and the second is an icon of the divine that relates, in apocalyptic tonality, the systems of oppression in the modern order.[26] By speaking in the margins, these two pieces call into question the limits of the modern theological discourse that Ruether uses in the center of the book to move us toward a feminist theology. It is as if we must use modern theology to correct the order and then must call into question the very tools of such correction.

Elisabeth Schüssler Fiorenza, more explicitly than most other feminist theologians, concentrates on forming discourses of emancipatory transformation from the marginality of women through her methodological work in biblical studies and feminist theology. One of the most interesting examples of her intentional nudging and playing with discourse is "The 'Quilting' of Women's History: Phoebe of Cenchreae."[27] In this article Schüssler Fiorenza weaves together two discourses, that of the historical method with that of a folk poem, to arrive at a new model for historical study. Schüssler Fiorenza introduces the notion of quilting by arguing for a strategy of replacement, substituting the model of the objective historical reporter who has command of the facts and can thus parallel historical reality with the model of the historian as a quilt maker who fits "together the surviving scraps of historical information into an overall design that gives meaning to the individual pieces."[28] Through a listing of principles of suspicion, including the admonition not to take masculine language at face value, Schüssler Fiorenza begins a skillful transformation of the "objective" historical method into a rhetorical method modeled after quilt making. Citing at length the historical "reality" of the development of patriarchy she uses this historical data to recast Phoebe as a Christian leader. Schüssler Fiorenza has provided us with a quilt that is a skillful account of the possible reality of that biblical account as seen from the situatedness of our own historical frame. What allows the strategy of replacement to become in reality a process of transformation is Schüssler Fiorenza's turn to rhetoric to design anew the status of historical discourse. As Schüssler Fiorenza explains,

> Reconstructive inferences, selection of evidence, and ascription of historical significance depend not only on the choice of explanatory

> models but also on the rhetorical aims and interests of the work. History is not written for people of past times but for the people of today and tomorrow.[29]

With this brief invocation of rhetoric, the historical reporter becomes a quilt maker, one who quilts for the dominant groups, "Far from recording with utmost objectivity 'what actually happened,' historians have written history for the dominant groups in society."[30] By first replacing then transforming the model of historical discourse from objective historian to quilt maker, Schüssler Fiorenza opens up the possibilities of plurivocity and multiplicity in discourse, and requires the recognition of the historicity of all discourse.

A third illustration is the discursive play of Catherine Keller's *From a Broken Web.* Spinning is an appropriate metaphor for Keller's practice, as she leads us almost breathlessly through the founding myths of Greek, Hebrew, and Christian culture, the depth psychologies of Freud and Jung, the philosophical anthropologies of Aristotle, Aquinas, Reinhold Niebuhr, feminist revisionism, and process philosophy to spin new images for an ontology of the self.[31] The text works by spinning layers of myths, philosophies, psychologies, and theologies of separateness and destructiveness to find the gentle-strong web of connectiveness that is already there. Clearly philosophical, the argument works best, in fact, on the level of a centrifugal force that provokes new images. But if, through the spinning of discourses, new images are provoked, others are seemingly spun "off," and the reader is transformed, mysteriously, into a self that though somewhat ethereal, is nonetheless freed from the twin afflictions of separation and domination.

All three of these feminist writings are certainly about emancipatory transformation, all want to free woman to speak, but to do so they must transform language itself. As feminist discourses they work in and through an emancipatory transformation of language and discourse, by providing new images (Keller's web, Schüssler Fiorenza's quilt), by multiplying the ways of speaking (Schüssler Fiorenza's rhetoric, Ruether's icon of apocalyptic dismantling), and by transforming the signifying practices of language in which otherness is not the taboo border but the generative margin for speaking and hearing (Ruether's beginning and ending with two different genres, Schüssler Fiorenza's interpretation of Phoebe through leading principles that blend quilting and historical scholarship, Keller's critique of the patriarchal order by spinning off images of separation and destruction and spinning new images of connection and transformation).

Emancipatory Transformation and Proclaiming the Word

In the production of these discourses of emancipatory transformation, feminist theologies proclaim the Word of God to and for the world. This is not to append some theological foundation or to annex a neoorthodox slogan of belief to feminist theology but, rather, to render explicit what is going on theologically in the discursive practices of feminist theology. For the discourses in feminist theology have to be understood in a Christian context as nothing less than speaking productively the Word through experience, community, Scripture, and tradition in and for the world today. Elisabeth Schüssler Fiorenza has stated this quite succinctly:

> feminist theologies introduce a radical shift into all forms of traditional theology, for they insist that the central commitment and accountability for feminist theology is not to *the* church as a male institution but to women in the churches, not to *the* tradition as such but to a feminist transformation of Christian traditions, not to *the* Bible as a whole but to the liberating word of God finding expression in the biblical writings.[32]

To understand and name feminist discourses as proclamations of the Word to and for the world is to attend to their theological reconstruction of the good news for this day and age but also to underscore the transformation of the basic terms of the social-symbolic order through new signifying practices.

Three reasons can be given to formulate feminist discourses of emancipatory transformation as discourses that proclaim the Word for and to world. First, feminist theology is not a mere corrective enterprise in Christianity. Rather, it is a reformulation of Christianity in which, among other things, the good news of Christianity emancipates and transforms the world, instead of, as was so often the case in modern Christianity, merely interpreting Christianity to itself.[33] If the Word as incarnate Word indicates the constructive formation of Christian witness in a historical period, then certainly feminist theology proclaims the living Word through its discourses of emancipatory transformation. Second, since the theological reconstruction of Christianity occurs in feminist theology through the multiplication of signifying practices and the formation of new discourses, a concentration on proclaiming the Word gives us a certain linguistic-theological access to the relations of God and world. Theology is, after all, words about God, and when God is spoken of as the Word then theology must include linguistic self-reflexivity on how we speak of God and world.[34] Third, what is especially startling about the production of feminist discourses as proclamations is that the relation of Word and woman has been so fundamental to her marginality. That feminist theology makes its constructive contribution as proclamation by linguistically multiplying discourses and making discourse work through signifying practices of multiplicity and otherness, is itself nothing short of an emancipatory transformation of Christianity's domination of women. Precisely as proclamation, feminist theology challenges the repression and otherness of woman as a collective singular set apart from the Word as the unique center of Christian community.

But is this notion of proclaiming Word to world helpful for feminist theology and will it add anything to feminist discourses of emancipatory transformation? Yes, for three reasons. First, by unveiling the linguistic and discursive practices of feminist theology as the form and substance of the Word in the present situation, feminist theology is no longer for women only and a few interested men, but intrinsic to Christianity and Christian witness in the world. Second, by locating the crux of feminism in the relations among the Word, words, and women, traditional theological loci such as Scripture, church, and witness to the world can be reconsidered with feminist theology determining the form, shape, and substance of theological reconstruction and not, as is so often the case, with modern theology providing the terms for adaptation, refutation, and correction. As proclaiming the Word, feminist theology no longer has to argue for a room for itself within the house of modern theology, but is free to build its own dwelling. Put in another fashion, feminist theology no longer has to rein in its power to the confines of modern theology, but is now set free in its power to open up the Scriptures, church, and witness in relation to its own proclamation of God. Finally, while the theological reconstruction that feminist theology offers is one of openness and not closure, distinct terms, values, and norms emerge to guide feminist discourse. That is to say, though feminism is a practice of resistance and transformation, it is not one of indeterminate anarchy. When the discourses of feminist theology are understood as proclaiming the Word of God, such discourse can be understood to be guided by the terms of specificity, difference, solidarity, embodiment, anticipation, and transformation.[35] These terms play continually throughout feminist discourses of emancipatory transformation, naming the signification of Word, the relation of words and Word in women's lives, and the process as well as the goals of feminist discourses. It is the privileging of these terms as constitutive of the Word that enables feminist discourses to be discourses *of* mulitiplicity and otherness and not just discourses *about* multiplicity and otherness.

In the space created by understanding feminist theological discourses as proclaiming Word to and for world and understanding proclamation in terms of feminism's emancipatory transformation it is also the case that feminism and Christianity find the most substantial promise for rending and renewing the social-symbolic order.[36] For here, in the outer margins of the transformation of Christianity, emerges an equally fascinating transformation, discourses that seek to rend and renew—by questioning, interrupting, correcting, and subverting the basic terms of the order—the signification of language, the ordering of subjectivity, the practices of reading, the modern configuration of time and space. Through multiple practices in writing and speech that invoke the God behind God, the Word hidden in words, feminist theology creates possibilities of emancipatory transformation for all. By pushing, shoving, blending, and fighting the margin as the limit, border, and edge, feminist theology promises a rending and renewing of the social-symbolic order.

To configure feminist discourses of emancipatory transformation as proclamations of the Word to and for the world is a constructive attempt in feminist systematics—to use the odd confluence of the new language of feminism with the older aspects of systematic theology. Systematic theology, as the creative, productive imaging of Christian faith, perhaps needs to be renamed to detach it from an ethos of idealism, but the imaging of Christian faith needs to be given effort and attention. There is a temptation today, when the threats to survival and flourishing are great, to lay down work and play with words to engage in what is often called "activism." Yet some of the greatest activism comes in renaming the world with new words, or words used in new ways.[37] Theology's purpose always has included a great deal of attention to words, images, and significations. Indeed, Augustine's famous treatise on how to interpret the Scriptures, entitled *On Christian Doctrine,* establishes a signifying principle of enjoying things that are eternal, or things that can be used to get to the eternal, and dismissing those to be loved for themselves.[38] Though Augustine's ordering is significantly different from that of modernity's, the point is that what we desire and what we enjoy are created or at least ordered through the use of signs. That which we love and desire is given to or arrived at through the ordering we employ, an ordering that, as Augustine suggested throughout his work, affects our reading of Scripture, our life in community, and our testifying to the world. It is this ordering, these signifying practices, and these ways of reading, of being in the church, and of speaking to the world, that must be reconstructed. For one of the greatest political (as well as linguistic and psychic) needs of the day is to speak to and of what we love, and what, in a world of destruction and death, we know as beautiful.

But Can Women Speak?

The discursive practices of feminist theology proclaim the Word to and for the world, a proclamation based on the belief that God appears today in the margins and gaps of our social-symbolic order manifest in terms of embodiment, solidarity, difference, anticipation, and transformation. Yet here we must ask, What is the theological possibility for such a proclamation? What is the nature of the Word that might allow, open up, grace, or in any way birth such a proclamation of the Word in emancipatory transformation? What is the nature, being, process of the Word that might fund terms such as difference and specificity, solidarity, transformation, embodiment, and anticipation? How does Word, and correlatively God, create emancipatory transformation as the process and aim of feminist discourses?

It is with this question that a great difficulty appears, for the Word has not been that which funds specificity, difference, embodiment, solidarity, anticipation, and transformation. Rather, the Word is that which has added a transcendental guarantee to the modern terms of identity, self-preservation, hierarchy, autonomy, and progress. The difficulty is compounded when woman is juxtaposed to Word, for woman has, in the discourses of Christianity, little or no access to the Word. Indeed both Word and woman may be said to limit the order: the Word is the limit of the order as its eternal guarantee, its autonomous preservation, its concern for sameness, certainty, and stability grounded beyond the heterogeneity of human life and language, while woman is the other, border of chaos and the sublime, taboo body, necessary womb, nurturer, mother, whore, and witch. If it is difficult to speak of the Word that funds mutuality and otherness, it is even more difficult to believe that such a Word might come from the voices, bodies, and lives of women.

Yet this is the problem, this relation of Word and woman, that must be confronted. The very precondition for the possibility of women speaking freely lies in the relation of women to the Word, a relation which, when opened for emancipation and transformation, requires a new discourse of the Word. Indeed, an emancipated relation between women and words rests on what has until now been experienced in the unnamed and the unnameable, the silences and the silencing, the hidden and repressed journey of women with the Word. Only if the Word can reveal itself in woman's marginality from which women now speak, as something other than master identity, primal referent, and governor of the governed, will feminist theology find a new Word and new words.[39] At the heart of women's future rests this wager and this risk: that there is today a Word not only of order but also of love, not only of law but also of grace. If this is possible, then feminist theology can hear the Word anew and proclaim the grace of freedom, not from the Word that thunders down on bent backs with a no to women's desires, but with the Word that speaks through women, in multiple and different fashions, in difference and specificity, for a yes of emancipation and transformation.

The reconstruction of the Word might begin with the common problem in feminist theory and practice of women's access to language; a problem that usually calls attention to the inability of language —indeed, perhaps its unwillingness—to give voice to women's experience.[40] Indeed, feminist theology in its most recent version was born in the inability of certain contemporary theologies to represent woman's experience, the experience of being a woman in a time in which the theology was understood as reflection on "common" human experience. The problem is not simply language's reflective capacities, but also its constitutive capacities, language's creation of woman through a character of division, a division creating and re-creating the basic division of male and female ordered always on the invocation of God, the primal signifier as the Word from which all words take order and meaning. It is, therefore, not enough to think of woman and words alone, for woman's access to language, in the historical discursive practice of patriarchy, is linked directly to her access to the Word.

The configuration of woman and Christianity is an intricate, complicated and even sorrowful historical construction. One way of following this history is by examining the founding of the monotheistic community on the Word, a Word which excludes woman from direct access to the heart of the community and secures the link of Word and man by allowing only men the representative activity of speaking for God.[41] Christianity claims over and over that the church is founded on Christ and is not dependent on any worldly reality, but in actual fact it depends on women's bodies to give it its saints and sinners. It was the Word/God that divided the sexes, and established the war of desperate need between them. It is, time and time again, God's Word that women are not allowed to represent. Why is it that women are not to speak in public of God, why is it a disgrace for women to represent God—except precisely that they present the physical body, and the relation of women's bodies to language, of language to bodies, of words to bodies in connections, in plurivocity, in openness, a relation of bodies and language against a Word that stands over, a Word that towers above?

Theologically, woman has been placed outside of words, in order to continue the funding of words through the Word, the words of the sociopolitical realm, but also the words of the natural, symbolic, and supernatural realms. There is a provocative power to Julia Kristeva's reading that monotheism, Western culture, and the marginality of women are woven tightly together, for the Word founds the community only by repressing the physicality of woman's body, relegating her to being outside of words and Word:

> Divided from man, made of that very thing which is lacking in him, the biblical woman will be wife, daughter or sister, or all of them at once, but she will rarely have a name. Her function is to assure procreation—the propagation of the race. But she has no direct relation with the law of the community and its political and religious unity: God generally speaks only to men. Which is not to say that woman doesn't know more about Him; indeed, she is the one who knows the material conditions, as it were, of the body, sex and procreation, which permit the existence of the community, its permanence and thus man's very dialogue with his God. Besides, is the entire community not the *bride* of God? But woman's knowledge is corporal,

> aspiring to pleasure rather than tribal unity (the forbidden fruit seduces Eve's sense of *sight* and *taste*). It is an informulable knowledge, an ironic common sense (Sarah, pregnant at ninety, laughs at this divine news); or else, when it serves social necessity, it's often in a roundabout way, after having violated the most ancient of taboos, that of incest (Sarah declared the sister of Abraham; Lot's daughters sleeping with their father).[42]

God founds community, thus funding language, by placing the divine Word, the Word of command and demand, as the only and ultimate foundation, the only source of real life. This repressive and illusory act creates human community by denying its embodiment, its continuity, its earth, and its own solidarity. Thus the Word must cast out woman, who represents the repressed preconditions of community and language: embodiment, difference, specificity, solidarity, anticipation, transformation.[43] In this fashion woman becomes a collective singular, as does man, and the hierarchical ordering of binary oppositions is the offspring of the forbidden relations between Word and woman.

Yet the ordering of this primal Word that founds community from outside of history is itself a figuration of Word, a figuration always ordered through the dominant discourse. For this Word which has denied access of women to words and Word, has itself been depleted, emptied, made an idol in current practice. Here Word is forced to re-present man's intent: the referent of man, the securer of his infinite freedom, his universal autonomy. In this way the Word itself has suffered: Word has been separated, time and time again, from its fullness and denied its solidarity with creation (which it, after all, created as the bridge of chaos and order), its embodiment in incarnation, and its rhythm of resurrection and crucifixion.

There is, however, pushing against the Word which has dominated our ordering, and ordered the domination, another reality of Word, known to women on the margins of the order. This is a reality of Word as creative, interrupting, and transforming process—of Word that bridges chaos and creation, bringing light, earth, animals, plants, woman, man, into physical being. This Word is the possibility behind a Word of order, of rule. This is the Word that is the matrix of all living things, bringing them out of chaos, across the abyss the order so fears, into life—a life of constant interweaving of day and night, of warmth and cold, of sunshine and rain. This Word is embodied, it comes not as a fortress against physical existence, but in, through, and out of our bodies—a Word incarnate that does not *put on* life as treasure in earthen vessels, but rather *is* earth, water, life.

This Word, peeking through the patriarchal discourses, escaping from women's bodies, setting the preconditions as margin of the Word of the order, bridges creation and transformation.[44] As creation it is embodied, it is both ground and abyss, it brings us into our differences and yet it creates differences together, in solidarity. As transformation, it is incarnate, the iconoclastic shattering of all finalities and the resurrection into new life, promise, and anticipation. This Word, which today gives vision and power, has dwelled with women on the margins of the order; it has enabled women to sing and to praise, to weave and to laugh, to love and to surround. It is the Word which creates and transforms, which calls into question and fashions anew.

This is not only a myth of woman's otherness, for it also speaks of woman's constant relation to language: outside, yet always the condition of the inside; providing the conditions of continuity but always and only through the discontinuity of having no direct access to Word; remaining in pleasure and in taboo. The margin outside of Word also suggests woman's relation to language—intimate yet forgotten; the ground, yet never expressed; creative, yet fallen in sin. The underground theological workings of language can be seen in certain French feminist theory where woman's relation to language is symbolized through the pre-oedipal vocalizations.[45] Here the feminine is written in the gaps, slips, and margins of language, indicating the precondition of language seen only as it breaks through its repression. This discourse of woman speaking her body, that is, of speaking the repressed ground of language itself, including discourses about the Word, reminds us that language, too, is physical. Language covers, as do women, the boundaries of nature and culture; symbolic in itself, it transcends its very conditions even as it must draw from them to represent transcendence.[46]

In the awesome recognition of the repressed relation of woman and the Word, a relation known in the splitting of otherness, it must be remembered that while woman is the fallen ground, the repressed desire of the Word, women also speak, and have spoken, in religious discourse. Denied public roles, separated from access to the Word of God, women have found discourses that speak of their desires and loves, that express their journey unto God within a Word not recognized by the

Word. The knowledge of this Word in relation to women is hidden in the readings of the Scriptures, in the prayers of women, in communities and communal relations women have formed, and even within the discourses Christianity has provided for women. It is not accurate to say that the discourses of Christianity, along with its communities and its Scriptures, have been entirely harmful to women. Such discourses as those of the Virgin Mary and of the cult of womanhood have provided for women positions in which to live, breathe, love, have children, paint, dream, and speak.[47] These discourses have been repressive and oppressive: they have forced, often in romantic idealistic terms, woman into modes of caretaking and selected her to play out sacrifical love. Yet these discourses also hint at a Word beyond and beneath the Word of governance, command, and law, a Word of plurivocity, embodiment, and connection.

What is it that requires law, order, governance, commands? Is this Word of body and earth, of connection and transformation, of difference and specificity, not the precondition for the Word of the order? Underneath the order, what is the substance that so fearfully stands in need of order, what is the frontier that must have boundaries, the limitless chasm that must be rimmed? Is there in this Word of body and earth, of creation and transformation, a limitless possibility that joins with the limitless possibility that is repressed in woman's marginality? If the Word of the order must make itself so strong and so powerful, what power is it resisting, except that of this other Word, hidden, repressed, expelled? The Word of creation and transformation is intimately linked with woman as the precondition for the possibility of the social-symbolic order.[48]

This Word has been shackled and hidden, ignored because of its openness to difference and specificity, denied because of its solidarity and embodiment, oppressed because of its plurivocity and fluidity. The Word as primal referent and patriarchal voice is, in modernity, the ultimate linguistic mirror of the social-symbolic order, God's warrant to the individual autonomous self who controls and masters all differences and desires.[49] On the one hand, then, God keeps the very materiality of women's speech repressed; on the other, women have found the dominant categories questionable in terms of their speaking of God, of their words and Word. Yet in the space of women's speaking—which is at the same time the space of the repression of the Word—lies the possibility of discourses of emancipatory transformation, the open possibility of transformation, of a freedom not only *from* the repressive ordering of patriarchy, but a freedom *for* creating, receiving, and reinventing new ways of speaking. In the space created among the Word, words, and women is the open possibility of change and transformation, not only in metaphors and concepts but in the ordering of language itself. The Word in which women speak their words moves against the social-symbolic order precisely in its movement against the monotheism of Word as primal referent and patriarchal voice.

The Word as the Perfectly Open Sign

The Word of creation and transformation, the Word of wisdom and song, the Word of solidarity and difference, is the possibility and wager of feminist discourses. It is necessary to speak of this Word as fully as possible, for only by doing so can Word, women, and words weave together emancipatory transformation. Women can speak when Word and words are open to them; existing in openness and solidarity, enabling and provoking women's ability and desire to speak. From the position of women speaking, Word opens out into its fullness, into the plenitude of its manifestation, into the multiplicity of language and discourse. For words of women, this Word blesses openness, the ability to bestow meaning but also to point forward to new meaning with both specificity and solidarity.

We need to present the theological possibility, despite the difficulties entailed, in a substantive fashion.[50] For this Word, this reality and image of Word that has been the repressed precondition for Word of the order, that has been and is the Word bridging nature and culture in women's bodies, that has existed in the ambiguities of Christian discourses about women, is the theological possibility of proclaiming good news in the world today. An explicit account of this Word is required for a basic orientation to feminist discourses, as the "precondition" of the possibility of discourses of emancipatory transformation. In this manner, Word names the multiplicity in and of feminist discourses by opening up the possibilities for multiple voices and for the multiplicity of every voice. Likewise, such a theological naming of the Word brings otherness, long taboo, into the very nature of Word, and into the nature of words. Thus, envisioning the signifying process of language by renaming the funding of discourse in Word to and for the world, blesses the plenitude of possibilities today emerging in the openness of women's lives. Moving from our reading of feminist discourses as marginal discourses that push, shove, rupture, and transform the order, it allows us to speak of the conditions for the possibility of play of and in feminist discourses, for the needs and reality of poetry, song, utopia, icons, spinning—all as legitimate speaking of Word to and for world.[51]

While the relation of Word and words can be said to pattern theologically the relation of God and world in discourses of emancipatory transformation, the immediate tasks are more narrowly those of theological semiotics and theological pragmatics: to identify the linguistic working of words in relation to Word (the task of theological semiotics) and to designate the logic of Word and discourse in feminist proclamations (the task of theological pragmatics).[52] Basic to what women will say in the discourses of emancipatory transformation is how they shall say it, for the possibilities of speaking of freedom may depend, at least in part, upon learning and being graced to speak freely. The values, attitudes, visions, and practices of emancipatory transformation must be born and reborn in the very process of women speaking and thus the Word must become incarnate in words to speak freely of freedom.

Theological semiotics identifies how to speak freely, or to say it another way, how the signifying process of language works. Theological semiotics can be developed through attention to signs as open, transformative and heterogeneous. To speak freely means, here, that words themselves are fixed neither by their essences nor by their self-referentiality, but by their context, the cultural practices in which they are used, by the interest of the persons using them, and by one sign's relation to other signs.[53] Signs, as Charles Peirce argued, anticipate new meaning, and are inherently transformative, open to new signification.[54] The plurivocity of signs, in feminism's theological semiotics, may offer the greatest resistance against the oppression of totalitarian discourses and practices. In the plurivocity of a feminist theological semiotics, the Word that guides discourse is imaged as the perfectly open sign.[55]

As the perfectly open sign we may say what Word is, in our best approximation, but also how it sustains the process of speaking. Here the Word is not that which breaks into discourse, or one that governs it, rather it is the full inclusivity of discourse; it creates and restores speech, it both allows symbols to have meaning and pushes against any fixed meaning. The Word/God is the sign of all signs, connected, embodied, open, multivalent, all the things a sign can most perfectly be, but the Word/God is this in the perfection of all perfection and thus, in full openness, creativity and gracefulness creates, sustains, and redeems all words in their ongoing process of signification. This means that words for Word are always doubly symbolic, or what I will call fully significant, for they not only symbolize other words, they always symbolize the full negation of such words, or, to say it differently, words for Word signify both the heterogeneous capacity of language as well as the ordering capacity.[56]

The twin side of this, from Word/God's side so to speak, is that the Word and words have between them a relation, but a relation that covers an impossible gap, an abyss of naming. Word/God is in a religious sense unnameable, God is not God's proper name, or as biblical tradition would have it *Yahweh* means "I am who I am," or as appropriate to our pragmatic style, "I will be who I will be."[57] There is not a literal name of God, a correspondence of God with a reality which in any positive sense signifies God. There are numerous ways to examine this claim, but, for our purposes, we will borrow the argument of Kenneth Burke in *Rhetoric of Religion*. Burke argues that there are four realms to which words apply: the natural, the sociopolitical, the symbolic (words about words), and the supernatural.[58] Burke names the human "the symbol user" since to create and use symbols is the human's natural, material existence, coming from nature even as it transcends nature.[59] The first three realms cover everyday experience but do not constitute all words. There are also those words which describe the transcendence of words, the realm of the supernatural, or as Burke says, "The supernatural is by definition the realm of the 'ineffable.' And language by definition is not suited to the expression of the 'ineffable.' "[60] For the sake of the present argument this means that the Word is "named" through words which, in return, may be borrowed to make new meanings for other words; the Word never reflects a correlative or corresponding reality of words. The relation between Word and words is one of meaning, presence, and signification, but also one of gaps, inexpressibility, rupture, and chaos. The nature of this relation may be transcendence, but it is a transcendence formed by a connection, the connection of discourse as the bridge between source and abyss.[61] There is, to use the Protestant Reformers' solution to this problem, always a hidden Word behind and beyond any revealed word.

The Word cast as perfectly open sign has, of course, some analogies that may help us image this notion, provided we remember Burke's warning that words cannot fully name the ineffable. There are many analogies to the notion of perfectly open sign, but four will serve to illustrate the linguistic analogy with other referents. First, there is the analogy between Word as perfectly open sign and the lives of women once women realize they do not have to be confined to the definitions given them in the social-symbolic order. Carolyn Heilbrun, for example, in a chapter in *Writing a Woman's Life,* examines how growing older is potentially a quite liberating experience for women. Against widely held views of the older women's life as nearly finished, done with life's work of marrying and raising a family, Heilbrun suggests that only in the older years of their lives do many women have the opportunity to be who they want to be. Heilbrun quotes an Isak Dinesen character saying, "Women when they are old enough to have done with the business of being women and can let loose their strength, must be the most powerful creatures in the world."[62] To understand the Word as the perfectly open sign is to receive the same startling revelation of possibility and openness, the transformation of categories and the manifestation of power as let loose in the lives of older women.

There is a contemporary theological image that also offers an analogy to the Word as perfectly open sign, that of the open history of the Trinity. Jürgen Moltmann, for example, has proposed a kind of narratology of God with the Trinity as the central theme which is open to "man" and history.[63] Within the narrative, Moltmann creates the Trinity as relational and open. That is, the Trinity includes the suffering of God—the suffering of the grieving Father and the suffering of the abandoned Son—yet this suffering also includes the sending of the Spirit to bring forth a new creation. Moltmann speaks of the open event of the Trinity and calls the Trinity a social event to signify, in narrative fashion, the relationality and openness of God within God's self and with the world. What is helpful about Moltmann's narratology is the relation of suffering and openness, for suffering does not create openness nor openness depend on suffering, but rather what happens with suffering, including the memories of those who have suffered in history, is an open possibility in the trinitarian history of God. Indeed, the relationship of openness and suffering in Moltmann's narratology of God has parallels to the theme of open history in many liberation theologies, wherein history itself is open to new creation in relation to the dangerous memories of suffering.[64]

The third analogy is the poem "For Strong Women," by Marge Piercy, that begins this book. Piercy's poem progressively opens up the word *strong* through its stanzas by resisting and transforming the ordinary definitions of strong through an analysis of the concrete reality of a woman's life. Strong is rarely a word used to describe a woman's being, if applied it is usually to mark a peculiar attribute of an unusual woman. Men are strong, after all, because women are weak. For Piercy, strength, the raw power of physical might, is combined with emotional power: as the first stanza ends the woman "goes on shoveling with tears in her nose."[65] As the poem moves toward completion, the word strong is opened by the craving for love, and strong emotions: "A strong woman is a woman who loves strongly and weeps strongly and is strongly terrified and has strong needs." Finally the word strong, a word usually identifying individual strength, is opened to terms of solidarity and connection: "Strong is what we make each other." Piercy, after opening the term up through the physical, emotional, and psychological realities of a woman's life, questions the closure of our usual definition of the strong individual who does not fear: "Until we are all strong together, a strong woman is a woman strongly afraid." The analogy with Word as the perfectly open sign lies in the possibilities of the new realities and new meanings that exist through the concreteness of women's lives, in the midst of and through daily activities. In a manner similar to Piercy's development of the word strong through the concrete realities of a woman's life, the Word as the perfectly open sign is revealed in solidarity and connection, questioning the closure of women's lives.

A conceptual analogy, our fourth example, may be drawn between feminism's Word as the perfectly open sign and Charles Peirce's understanding of the signifying process. Signification is, for Peirce, fundamentally a process rather than a predetermined relation of sign to object. To understand the process, we must begin with the realization of its diachronic nature, that is, at any given time we can only try to accept the reality of all that has gone on and all that is projected.[66] We cannot simply bracket off or escape from the historicality of the signifying process. Peirce contends that the only state of mind one can begin with is "the very state of mind in which you actually find yourself at the time you do 'set out'—a state in which you are laden with an immense mass of cognition already formed. . . ."[67] The state of mind, for Peirce, is a product of signification, but it is always open to new meanings and interpretations. Though signification is an open process it is determined first as the product of past signification and second in terms of present relations; signification, for Peirce, is regulated through the anticipation of the real or the true in reference to the future community of investigators. The Word as perfectly open sign parallels the historicality of the signifying process: like signification, Word is a process and thus not fixed; it arises at all times, out of particular situations and thus anticipates possibilities through the present historical situation.

Word, as matrix and abyss of words, both guides and disrupts the signifying process. This hypothesis could have a multitude of implications, including the linguistic retrieval of traditional views of God's relation to the world. But our primary point, at this time, is that the Word funds words even as it constantly negates, pushes against, and sounds outside of them. In a sense, this is merely the first two commandments of theological discourse; Word will be the matrix, and no word will compete with or fully name the abyss of the Word. The Word as matrix and abyss is embodied in the words themselves, both as the constitution of language and as the disruption of language.

It is important to emphasize that though the Word as perfectly open sign works within feminist discourse to move against closure and to open up possibilities, it is an openness that comes through the realities of women's lives, their sufferings, desires, and pleasures. Furthermore, this openness of the Word working through the words and lives of women yields terms, the linguistic equivalent to values and norms, to guide feminist discourse. These terms arise in the interrelation of Word and women's words: they are the terms of a signifying process which is open to new possibilities and they are the values of women's lives expressed in feminist theology. These terms, arising from and returning to feminist discourse can be identified as solidarity, embodiment, anticipation, specificity, difference, and transformation.

The Word, as matrix and abyss, is in solidarity with words, meaning that the Word is with words, in words, but not controlling words. The Word does not come down from above but emerges and reveals itself within the embodied reality of women's lives. The solidarity and embodiment of the Word makes words free, the presence of the Word lets them be open, ambiguous, and meaningful. The first terms, values, and norms that the Word as perfectly open sign gives to theological discourse are *solidarity* and *embodiment,* terms of being with and being for, but being with and for in process. The Word both gives life to women's words and leads women's words to new life.[68]

The terms solidarity and embodiment within the Word as the perfectly open sign lead to the term *anticipation.* Words are never closed, freedom is never final, for in the open solidarity of Word and words, words are always pointing to that which they do not yet express. The Word, as a perfectly open sign, is not "behind" our words but is present-future in words, playing, anticipating, pointing to new forms of freedom.[69] The perfectly open sign of Word in a proclamation of emancipatory transformation means that all discourse anticipates, that it speaks in the present, drawing on words past, but always moving into new meanings, words, and experiences of freedom.

Solidarity, embodiment, and anticipation in the Word as the perfectly open sign lead us to the terms *specificity, difference,* and *transformation.* The perfectly open sign means that all signs, in relation to their connectedness, a connectedness of solidarity and anticipation, receive the integrity of their specificity and difference. Indeed not all words are one, nor is there any univocal meaning, thus words must be attended to in their specificity and difference, never finalizing them through oppositions, never stabilizing them through fixed hierarchies, but considering, creating, rending, and renewing them in new possibilities. In this manner the perfectly open sign funds words in the ongoing process of transformation, for only as specificity and difference meet embodiment, solidarity, and anticipation can transformation occur.[70] In this matter words can transform, as can words produce transformation.

The relation of Word and words, in proclaiming emancipatory transformation encompasses terms of solidarity, embodiment, anticipation, specificity, difference, and transformation. The Word as a perfectly open sign means, then, that feminist discourses, both their content and process, are filled with God's Word, incarnate in God's love, freeing and transforming words in solidarity with the world. A proclamation of emancipatory transformation, by act and by message, must be in solidarity with the world, it must speak of the restoration of the earth and the transformation of the order; it must be present with suffering and with hope. Women's words, always relating to Word as perfectly open sign, anticipate, claiming the present toward the future. Feminist discourses re-member the past for its redemption in the future; they move human subjectivity in the journey of becoming and not, as so often has been the journey of women, within endless variations on a pattern established long ago. Thus feminist discourses are, by this Word of freedom, also transforming discourses, hoping not only to call for change but to invoke it; transforming discourses not only about living anew but gracing new life into being. The Word as a perfectly open sign means that all proclamation lives, symbolically, with incarnation, passion, and resurrection.

Having identified the Word as perfectly open sign in relation to words in a feminist theological semiotics, it is important to designate feminism's theological pragmatics, the logic of meaning or the creation of meaning that emerges in relation to the signifying practices of women's words.[71] For how language works in feminist discourse also suggests certain ways of forming and guiding proclamations of emancipatory transformation, ways of bringing together women's voices with the stories of the Scriptures, and women's visions of freedom with the gifts of women-church. This logic, or theological pragmatics, can be designated through three leading principles.[72]

First leading principle: In a proclamation of emancipatory transformation, the logic of abduction guides the formation of feminist discourses.[73] The task of feminist theology includes the formation of new poetic practices and new rhetorics; therefore, feminist theology must construct, weave, and image new visions of human flourishing. Feminism, as a practice of resistance and transformation, is concerned with the making of new meaning, including new forms of subjectivity, language, and politics. In this process, itself a process of emancipatory transformation, feminism creates new visions and meaning through what the pragmatists called abduction, the procreation of meaning in the creative inference of new possibilities.[74] Abduction, as a signifying act, has been concealed through much of the signifying process as that which we just intuit, or as what just happens. But abduction, given the notion of Word/God as perfectly open sign and the rending and renewal of human practices from the position of margins and gaps in the social-symbolic order, places the priority of our poetics and rhetorics on creativity, the creation of the new from the present and the past. Proclaiming emancipatory transformation requires, in this time and place, not only deductive arguments, based on general premises in common, nor merely inductive premises drawing a common theme from singular cases, but also, and especially, abductive inferences and the creation of the new in particular and specific ways. Abduction is hypothetical, introducing new ideas, as compared to induction, which determines values, and deduction, which evolves the necessary consequences of a hypothesis.[75] As Peirce explained, "Deduction proves that something *must* be; induction shows that something *actually is* operative; abduction merely suggests that something *may be.*"[76] Abduction enacts, therefore, the desire for flourishing, the solidarity of our togetherness, and the anticipation of what is possible for each and for all.

Second leading principle: Abductive logic, in relation to Word as perfectly open sign, operates through the play of aesthetics in the imaging of human flourishing. To change both signifying practices and to form new discourses is a difficult task. Feminism must take the material, the ideas, the dreams women have and reimage them, building, redoing, creating anew, transforming what women envision as the beauty of human flourishing.[77] This process can be conceived of as a type of aesthetic "play," a sliding between the rules and the possibilities they repress and open up, a fashioning anew of the present possibilities in our lives.[78] This type of play is, as feminist critic Patricia Yaeger has noted, a border between sensuous and rational experience. In terms of moving amid language and discourses, play has, as Yaeger indicates, a liminal status, "It exists neither inside nor outside, neither bound by social rules nor free from them. . . . The area of playing is, in fact, the place where the opposition between a reality which is 'objectively perceptible and objectively knowledgeable' and a delirious inner reality breaks down."[79] It is when play emerges out of the abductive practice of language itself, that feminism may develop new images of human flourishing. These are, for the time being, aesthetic practices that will, hopefully, nurture and nourish, bringing into being new practices of subjectivity, language, and politics for all persons. The status of feminist discourses as types of aesthetic play is not humanistic, it does not rest on appeals to a metahistorical structure of full humanity which our language represents.[80] Rather, feminist discourses rest on the reconstruction of language itself through the relation of Word, words, and women, and appeals to visions of human flourishing in relation to the fundamental terms expressed in Word and words: solidarity, embodiment, difference, specificity, anticipation, and transformation.

Third leading principle: The movement of logic with aesthetics must always be in relation to rhetorical practices, that is the visions of God and human flourishing must coordinate with habits, actions, institutions in the realm of praxis, and intentional human activity.[81] This text follows the hunch that current habits, practices, and institutions cannot themselves be corrected enough to address the questions and crises of the cultural and world situation. Rather, contemporary habits, institutions, and practices contribute greatly to the need for discourses of emancipatory transformation. But such discourses have their worth, in human terms, only by way of impacting, pushing, revisioning, and dreaming new ways of being and doing in intentional human activity. Thus my insistence on discourses aimed at the shift of fundamental attitudes through the shift of deliberative practices is, by and large, a matter of emphasis. While I do think there are discourses of fundamental attitudes, these have, upon hearing, implications for intentional human activity, and likewise even the most technical discourses of deliberative practice hold within them views of human flourishing.[82] Even words that hold onto the realm of the supernatural, by the very nature of their source and location, carry possible consequences for praxis, and likewise all words within them carry some hope of the Word.

·2·

The Power of Freedom: Proclamation and Scripture

But over and against all this stand sentiments no other religious book contains: suffering that will suffer no longer; buoyant expectation of Exodus and restorative transformation —not in some Psalms of lowliness, but very definitely in Job, and elsewhere too. Piety here, from first to last, belongs to the restless alone; and the particular brand of Utopian loyalty which keeps him (sic) *restless is the only thing that is, in the long run, deep.*

Ernst Bloch

The question to be addressed in this chapter relating the Scriptures and proclamation is twofold: first, given the Word as perfectly open sign in feminism's theological semiotics and theological pragmatics, how do the Scriptures function in proclamation; and second, what do the Scriptures suggest about the nature of proclamation in the present context? These questions, though related to research in biblical hermeneutics, are pointedly theological, asking how feminist discourses that today proclaim the Word to and for the world use the Bible and are guided by the Bible.[1] Because the present concern is theological, and focuses on proclamation, questions of the biblical scholar in terms of historical or literary criticism will remain largely in the background, though resources from these perspectives will work their way into the text. Rather, this chapter considers how the Bible speaks to women, how it speaks of new visions, new hopes, new ways, and new actions; how it enables women to speak in multiple and diverse ways in discourses of emancipatory transformation.

The Scriptures are received and used in proclamation through the working of Word and Spirit. In feminist discourses the Word which moves within the Scriptures is not the Word behind all words, taking words on as empty vessels, nor is it a Word that reflects the autonomy of individual existence. It is, as the relation of women, words, and Word suggests, the perfectly open sign moving through, within, embodied, incarnate in words: signifying specificity, difference, mutuality, embodiment, anticipation, and transformation. Within the words of the Scriptures, the Word works to provoke, speak, anticipate, move, and point forward.

The Scriptures, enlivened by the Word as perfectly open sign, operate in the play of images, in the aesthetics of new visions of human flourishing: in the language of poetry, singing, dancing, praying, hoping, loving, desiring, and living. The Scriptures have been used, at times, to make a moral point or to give a lesson in good Christian sense; likewise they have been used to announce the wholly other.[2] In feminist discourse the Scriptures work through an aesthetic play of images to perform and produce emancipatory transformation. The Scriptures are used to embrace the hearer, to respect the hearer, to be in solidarity but also to point forward, and to anticipate transformation, both provoking and satisfying desires for freedom.

Such imaging, an aesthetic play of images within the Scriptures, occurs within the discourse and praxis of Christian community; to say it differently, images are born out of and speak to the rhetorical practices of Christian community. Piety and prayer, after all, live together in discourse, and images of ascent to God arise out of the habits and longings of daily life. From creation stories that show the relation of all to all, through the differences made by a God who brings life from nothing, to journeys of freedom, to possibilities of justice and peace, to communities born with tongues of fire so they may have the power to speak, stories give flesh to vision while vision performs the stories in the midst of daily life.[3]

In relation to the first question as to how the Scriptures function in proclamation, it is necessary to have both a formal answer concerning the status of the Scriptures and a material answer concerning the substance of the Scriptures. The formal answer is that feminist theology uses the Scriptures as collections of proclamations, as models of Christian discourses of emancipatory transformation.[4] The Bible speaks authoritatively within the Word in feminist discourse in regards to its credible claims of freedom: its stories, its visions, its images, its hopes, its failures, its history, and its future.[5] All feminist discourse must approach the Bible with suspicion for its contents are not "pure" discourses: the Scriptures themselves demonstrate the tragic distortion of speaking of freedom through the very configuration of woman as less than and "other" than man.[6] But these Scriptures have spoken to women and men throughout history through their credible claims of freedom, challenging, provoking, and making women and men see with new eyes of hope. In memory of those who have heard freedom through these Scriptures, and in solidarity with those who have suffered when these Scriptures have been used to belittle and abuse them, feminists read and hear these Scriptures not as empty vessels to be filled or as hidden riddles to be deciphered, but as proclamations, as the Word experienced and expressed in words of emancipatory transformation.[7] In this we follow Elisabeth Schüssler Fiorenza's notion that Scripture should be treated as a structuring prototype and not as an eternal archetype; as a model of how Christians have, rhetorically and aesthetically, proclaimed the Word in the world; as speaking to and with their communities and not as containing universal a priori rules of action or structures of existence.[8] In Schüssler Fiorenza's words:

> I have therefore proposed that we understand the Bible as a structuring prototype of women-church rather than as a timeless archetype, as an open-ended paradigm that sets experience in motion and structures transformations. Rather than reducing the biblical multiformity and richness of experience to abstract principles or impulses to be applied to new situations, I suggest the notion of a historical prototype open to its own critical transformation.[9]

Expanding upon Schüssler Fiorenza's notion of Scripture as prototype, feminist theology treats the Scriptures, in their multiplicity and plurivocity, as prototypes in order to examine them through abductive logic as models which guide reflection and action but are always open to transformation.

This means that the Bible can and must be considered in its entirety around the norms of revelation for the community.[10] It also means that the Bible is liberated from being translated only into moral rules or existential insights, and freed to express the multiplicity and otherness in its voices. As Schüssler Fiorenza explains, understanding Scripture as prototype rather than archetype "allows us to reclaim the Bible as enabling resource, as bread not stone, as legacy and heritage, not only of patriarchal religion but also of women-church as the discipleship of equals."[11]

Feminist theology, of course, must say more than this in a theology of proclamation, for feminists want not just to understand the Bible, but to proclaim God's Word in, from, and through it. The material answer to how women read the Scriptures arises from what we will call a feminist hermeneutics of marginality. Feminists read the Bible from the only place possible: cast, on the one hand, as the margin of the social-symbolic order and the margin of Christianity, and, on the other hand, receiving the words of the Bible as words of plenitude in the Word as perfectly open sign. As Schüssler Fiorenza has pointed out, women approach the Bible with suspicion, but also with proclamation, with memory but also with transformation.[12] Feminists must constantly read the Bible with a hermeneutics of marginality: receiving it as a monument of patriarchal oppression, but also knowing the Bible through its credible claims of freedom.

As feminists read the Bible for proclamation, they read it with women's knowledge, that is women's way of knowing in the Word. Here, enlivened by the Spirit of emancipation and of transformation, there emerge, even amid its androcentrism, credible claims of freedom for women. The notion of a hermeneutics of marginality necessitates that a feminist reading of the Scriptures ask where and how God is testified to among the others of history, as well as where and how God is expressed as condoning the oppression, the silencing, and the abuse of women. Especially in relation to proclamation, a feminist hermeneutics of marginality attempts to find those discourses in the Bible that speak of emancipatory transformation, including those discourses which scholars have neglected or misread due to their own sexism.[13]

A feminist hermeneutics of marginality includes more than just an open dialogue about freedom, more than just an identification of discourses that elevate women, more than just an examination of and opposition to the discourses that devalue women. It also includes new practices of reading: the pushing, shoving, and playing with the texts themselves as transformative discourses. It includes the theological reading of the Word though these words, of reading with the Bible through the privileging of difference, specificity, embodiment, mutuality, transformation, and anticipation. In these ways the dialogue between the Scriptures and feminist reading is one of openness, even restlessness. A feminist hermeneutics of marginality emphasizes reading itself as an experience of emancipatory transformation.

Finally, a feminist hermeneutics of marginality entails the reading of the Scriptures in light of the present critique and transformation of the social-symbolic order. The marginality of women gives eyes to see not only the status and role of women, but a view of the social-symbolic order: its institutions, principles, organization of space and time, hidden rules, and ideologies. Feminism does not, in the hermeneutics of marginality, suspend the interpretation of women's present situation in reading the Scriptures. Indeed, the historical situation provides the avenue into the Scriptures, as the Scriptures shed light on the situation. In the hermeneutics of marginality, the Scriptures are read for the Word in these words, and what Word and words say by way of criticism, explanation, announcement, questioning, affirmation, comfort, and transformation of the present situation.[14] The Scriptures, read through the Word, serve as they have in many times and places of Christianity: to provide insight and images to speak of sin, distortion, and oppression as well as good news, grace, and salvation.

Combining the formal principle of the Scriptures as prototypes with the material principle of a hermeneutics of marginality, the feminist understanding of the Scriptures exists amid the incarnation of Word in words; these historical models engage a play of meaning and vision so that women may speak anew of emancipatory transformation. The Scriptures have a "special" status because of beliefs internal to Christianity, beliefs which are reconstructed in various historical periods. Christianity has tried a number of ways of speaking about the Scriptures as special revelation using notions such as God's authorship and the presence of Spirit and Word.[15] In the present context, the Scriptures are "sacred" because, in relation to community and to feminist discourses of emancipatory transformation, they are stories of people seeking to speak of freedom, many times failing, many times only vaguely glimpsing the Word freeing their words, but nonetheless providing both visions of freedom and models of proclamation to receive and to refashion. Yet the Scriptures, for the Christian community, are not smaller versions of master narratives that either swallow up or represent experience, but are prototypical relations of Word and words, for the Scriptures are proclaimed by the vibrancy of Word and word in them, enlivened by the Spirit. The Spirit—God present, never tamed—works between the Scriptures, the community, and the world. Scriptures are thus "sacred" not because they are connected with Christianity and thus have to be holy, but because through the Scriptures, in the power of Word and words, Christians speak to sanctify the world, offering the visions, attitudes, images, narratives, and poetry to restore the world to transforming grace.

The Scriptures and experience are thus part of proclamation, not the goal of Christianity interpreting itself to itself. Scriptures may be constitutive of Christian community, and Christian community enlivened by its Scriptures, but both together are for the world, for both together make up the discourses of emancipatory transformation that today constitute the Word in and for the world. The Scriptures are neither the origin nor the telos of Christianity; the Scriptures and community live amid the ongoing relation to Word and words in proclaiming God's Word. Thus, the Scriptures are decentered in proclamation, but because of proclamation the Scriptures also decenter the Christian community in relation to Word and world.

Given how the Scriptures function as prototypes through a hermeneutics of marginality, our second question can be addressed: What do the Scriptures say of proclamation? In order to address this question, one scriptural text can be examined, one that receives through the Word the Spirit of freedom as it gives to the Word embodiment in time and space, persons and place, passion and action. Such a sample is not the "origin" of discourse nor even the prototype of prototypes, but one, rather, drawn from the faltering speech of the movement between text and life, one which can be known and yet cannot be contained in the limits of that knowledge.

Luke 4:16–30 speaks of freedom: the freedom to survive, to have food, to be set free from the chains of injustice, to use the world's resources for curing injustice rather than making war, for healing and wholeness, for good news. It is not a forgotten text in the contemporary world; preached from, spoken of, longed for, this text speaks to the world and to the church. To Christianity, it is invoked as mission and piety, as what Christianity should and must be about to be true, to be loyal to God, Christ, Spirit, Scriptures, and tradition. Prophetically invoked, this text is often used to speak for God, to call people back to a mission given in Christ, a mission of justice and transformed relations. And in this mission, this prophetic critique and reinterpretation of Christianity, these words of Scripture proclaim to the world that the poor, the lame, and the captive are to be emancipated into the fullness and plurivocity of freedom to live again in creation, transformed into the fullness of human flourishing.

This text of Luke 4:16–30 is peculiarly apt since it is a persuasive discourse of and about emancipatory transformation. The text will be read through six questions about proclamation, all the while remembering that only one prototype is being examined, and receiving through this prototype the Word as perfectly open sign in the credible claims of freedom.[16] The first question will be, What is the locus of proclamation—time, space, place—and the location of proclamation this text models for us linguistically and theologically? The second question is, What is the process of the proclamation, what makes it proclamation, rather than mere announcement, information, or description? The third question follows logically from the second: What is the content of the proclamation, what claims are made, and what is it about? The fourth question asks, What is the point of proclamation? The fifth question considers the status of proclamation, that is, What does this text do with words and deeds in proclamation? Finally, the sixth and last question reverses this process and asks whether and how this scriptural text exceeds proclamation.

It is necessary to underscore that this is a theological reading, an open dialogue between contemporary feminist theology as discourses of emancipatory transformation and a model of Scripture as containing discourses of emancipatory transformation. Although Lucan commentaries and biblical scholarship are employed, this is an appropriation of Luke 4:16–30 to model, suggest, and form an understanding of what proclamation is in today's world given feminist theology's understanding of the Word. Such a reading combines insights into the text with insights into the situation; it moves, as do Christian lives, between text and experience, seeking not to translate the one into the other but to enrich both through the ongoing dialogue—a dialogue of openness—between the two.[17]

In this reading a feminist hermeneutics of marginality, which has been outlined above, is employed in a kind of sympathetic siding with the text, in an identification of proclamation as the reordering of relations. It is fair to say that in a feminist hermeneutics of marginality appropriation, the practical use of the text, becomes the emphasis of interpretive activity.[18] That is, the text is to be "used," made sense of, dialogued with rather than only explained, disclosed, and examined.

Indeed, it is the experience of feminist theology as offering discourses of emancipatory transformation that opens readers to this text; this text, in turn, will suggest how such discourses can be offered as proclaiming God's Word to the world. Perhaps the understanding of the Scriptures as prototypes will allow Christianity again to be intentional about the theological appropriation of the Bible. If the Scriptures are best understood as attempts by early Christian communities to appropriate tradition in order to address their current life situations, then feminist theology can create and discover warrants for theological appropriation. Tradition in this sense is to be used, to be passed on, and thus to be transformed, although, as shall emerge, this by no means requires that the text be entirely domesticated to present questions.

I speak as a woman, and although this passage is not directly about women I see in it a feminist vision, a vision of reordered relations, a vision of the power of testimony, a vision of free play and open connections. I will speak of this passage, for women can claim what they hear, and say what appears to them, in the power of the Spirit. To proclaim emancipatory transformation women are empowered to take back the Scriptures: to speak of them and to hear them, painfully, angrily, prophetically, hopefully, lovingly, and gracefully. In this manner Luke is especially helpful for he begins, as I hear the Word and words, by calling into question the very time, space, and identity of the order, and speaking for a very other place, a place of connection and rupture, of relations and hearing, a place which may be today the place of women.

The Time and Space of the Book

> And he came to Nazareth, where he had been brought up; and he went to the synagogue, as his custom was, on the sabbath day. And he stood up to read; and there was given to him the book of the prophet Isaiah. He opened the book and found the place where it was written. . . . (Luke 4:16–17)

The first question to ask of this text is what is the locus of proclamation—where does this text take place, what is the time and place of this text? It is, even at first glance, obvious that the place of this text is a communal one, the time and space that of Jesus' community. Neither community, nor book, nor Jesus is prior here, but all together, for that is the custom. A proclamation of emancipatory transformation begins, at least in this beginning, in a peculiar fashion: by setting it off in time and space, in voice and reading, in community and book. Indeed, even before the discourse begins a dislocation takes place, the time of God is invoked—the Sabbath Day—and the community which forms the discourse is formed not first by speaking but by hearing.

Furthermore, it is not just any community, but a synagogue, a place to read and to worship, to be and to act in the community of God's people. On the Sabbath he comes into the synagogue. The Sabbath is, within this text, configured through Jesus, community, and book. Proclamation begins, or is at least located, by the temporality of rupturing the daily ordering. For this day is different—different because it both connects the other days together in created glory and different because it calls into question those other days. Judaism understands this better than do we who configure the Sabbath with Jesus, for many Jews observe this day as set apart: doing differently, changing and letting go of the ordinary, reordering activity in a radical fashion. "Observing" Jews continue not only the custom of gathering and reading but also the habit of "observing" the day without ordinary work, be it cooking, constructing, or creating. Day-to-day temporality is revoked in the speaking of freedom in order to receive and recognize God's presence. Christians observe this day differently, observing it only as a day off from work, a day for rest from ordering and a rest for more ordering; for Christians the Sabbath serves the order rather than rupturing it for observation of the otherness that is greater than ordering.

Proclamation, in the calling out, the naming, the claiming for, involves the invoking of the temporality of God, a temporality that is not, at least in the space of this text, to be identified with the time of normal ordering, with the linear preseveration of our identities as being always in our control.[19] The time of work, of daily living, is governed by the clock. Against the control and mastery by this temporal ordering, the Sabbath beckons participants into cosmic time, the radical connectedness of all time, and kairotic time, the rupture of ordered time. Cosmic time is the temporality of relatedness, the ceaseless rhythms of "natural time," not progress toward an end, not cause from an origin, but an endless flow of connectedness. This temporal connectedness of God's time is experienced rarely in the modern world, for modernity orders the connectedness even in the very ordering of language. Yet in the experience of birthing, of nature, of prayer, whispers the temporality that all rests in God: the relatedness of the ebb and flow of children and mothers, body, interdependence, demanding, giving, the temporality of God and world; the nonstop reach of prayer finally lost, confessions given, intercessions offered, until one is finally with and not-with God; the prayer of the saints, pulsations within and beyond the ordering of words. Within this pulsating temporality, with both its discomfort and its assurance, the borders of the self are blended, fused, confused, yet the coming to be of the self cries, sings. This is pointed to in Friedrich Schleiermacher's configuration of the relation of God's providence to the feeling of absolute dependence: the temporality of being absolutely dependent must be of a cosmic connection that is always coming to be. Yet Schleiermacher himself has to "order" instead of "feel" by placing the individual consciousness in control and configuring history as the arena of God's providence ordered by men. Still the cosmic temporality makes its presence felt, for instance, in the dialogues on Christmas Eve where the location of women's experience is somehow "intuitive" of the religious, suggesting a knowledge of God beyond or other than that expressed in the ordered discourse of the men.[20] The Sabbath, in which Jesus comes, is cosmic time, the connectedness of time and proclamation, the time known within the heart and soul, time of ceaseless rhythm cascading into freedom for all the connectedness of God and world.

There is another sense of temporality to the Sabbath that stands apart from cosmic time even as it breaks into linear time; it is a time that is confronted as difference, as otherness. The Sabbath stands apart—not to be confined to the weekly ordering, the daily mastery of knowing, the worship of the clock. This is God's time and time here is GOD; the God that is first and last, the God that confronts, the God that is hidden in and beyond revelation; this is time exploded. Karl Barth tried to express this time—time of neither nature nor history—but modern readers could not hear, wanting the reception of revelation to order time as much as did the experience of Schleiermacher's connectedness of time.[21] Paul Tillich, too, points to time as *kairos*, as compared to time as *chronos*.[22] This time does not blend the borders of the self as much as it calls all borders into question. It is, quite simply, other time, time as other, the other as time. It is not easy to speak of this time, since nothing rests on it as it does in the way of cosmic time; this time presupposes nothing, but rather calls into question all that is presupposed. Yet it does break forth, admitting the possibility of radical change, radical chaos, radical openness. Perhaps it can be identified as the incredible openness of time; since any description of it can and would be exploited and exploded. Certain events hint at this time of time—Sinai, Resurrection, Pentecost—what is time in and of these events? Time here serves as the locus of proclamation as a claiming forth, a rupture of time itself, an interruption of order, progress, mastery—other time, time of God.

Cosmic time and kairotic time push, blend, bend, and obscure the boundaries of the normal ordering of time and, thus, of the time of the order. Discourses of freedom and about freedom must today invoke God's time, for only in this way can they both oppose modern time and offer alternatives to time as domination, mastery, and control. Modernity has thrived on clock time. What makes modernity possible except the very ordering of time? Time to begin and end, progress and process, time of minutes, hours, seconds, milliseconds. Yet even for modernity this time of progress and process has not been able to control and order all experience and knowledge. Modernity experienced something more, an experience of the self that was not completely orderable, manageable. So, within the basic rules of the modern game, rules that contain difference, at best, through a principle of a dialectic, modernity invented or stumbled upon the time of the individual, the negation of history as ordering, the ahistoricity of the existential self. This temporality, actually sort of an atemporality if temporality is defined solely as linear progression, assumes that one can flee from history, that one can bracket relations, that one can suspend connectedness, that one can forego events and ruptures, and thus and only thus, that one can find the true self. Theology tended to divide God's time between the two: the God of providence worked historical or metaphysical ordering in created time while the God of redemption evoked the existential moment over and over again in eternal time. Yet God's time didn't have equal status within the two times, for in the first, the time of history, God's time coexisted, riding along silently, with the historical process, keeping quiet in public, while, in the second, God's time was much more involved, provoking, evoking, demanding a decision of the private, existential individual.[23] The existential self, in modernity, was the private self, and religion a private affair; this redemptive religious time helped secure the fragile self who, in the contours of modernity, struggled somehow to say yes to existence. As the time of decision, religion and the private, unempowered self kept each other upright, for the ordering of time depended on the fragile self's ability to keep itself afloat. Existential time had no conflict with the time of progress, it was the inner lining of the cloak of the social-symbolic ordering of modernity.

The text locates proclamation in questioning the ordering of this time: on the Sabbath God's temporality calls persons into question, the temporality of connected rhythms of existence, a rhythm that is not posited as identity but as difference, a temporality that stands radically apart, disordering and disrupting the order. Indeed the locus of proclamation stands opposed to the time of modernity not by prophetic declaration of intent, but by a vision of time not that of linear order. The time of proclamation envisions connection and otherness, life without ceasing and life as other, God whose time is an expansion of God's relation to all and God whose time is not controlled through the ordering of words. Thus the community, or synagogue, does not and cannot entirely control and order time together; indeed, this Sabbath time, time of God from which to speak of freedom, decenters the progress of history as a collective singular and the existential of the individual as eternally present. The text of/on proclamation gathers persons now in God's time not as isolated individuals gathered to worship, not as atomistic selves sharing in common certain needs, goals, and desires, but in the locus of a community, group, body, called and instituted by God.

This is difficult to grasp or be grasped by for the common practice is to think of a community as a collection of atomistic individuals. Indeed modernity is as much marked by this spatiality of the differentiated self as by the temporality of history/ahistoricity. It is configured in practices of social groups and in the written work of Enlightenment philosophers.[24] The spatiality of the differentiated self governs the modern practice of churches as voluntary associations. The organization of churches as voluntary associations assumes that any problem of the relations between church and state is solved through an institutional practice of spatial differentiation between the secular public realm and the private religious realm. It is important to notice that such a separation is related to the belief that religiosity is already determined in the individual prior to any expression in space and time through organized religion. The space of community is constitutive neither for the individual believer nor for the public at large.

And so Jesus entered on the Sabbath, the time of God, into the synagogue, the community, as was his custom. It is not custom or habit as merely an individual quirk of repeated behavior, but the constitutive act of community and of the personal, the interpersonal and the communal; this constitutive act is a spatial measure, and space constitutes the coming, the going, the being there and the being with. Those who proclaim exist, communally and individually, in space and time, which requires the continual demand for interpretation and results in the impossibility of a final interpretation. There is never the finality of the pure community, nor the identity of the perfected self. Rather, proclaimers must be reminded constantly of the brokenness of discourse about God and about community/self existence. To reflect, speak, and act, those who proclaim must try to understand the spatiality and temporality of community.

It is with the expansiveness of time and space in the community that Jesus is given the book and reads. At the beginning of the proclamation, we, who desire to proclaim, are yet again decentered from ourselves, for now we do not speak first, but listen. The Scriptures are central to the setting, for proclaimers according to this text are readers of the Scriptures. As readers, proclaimers are in one way or another imitators of action and so are actors of the Scriptures. Jesus reads the Scriptures, is refigured by the Scriptures, interprets and lives the Scriptures.

We, as those who proclaim, are asked to listen to the Bible that, in some sense, makes us who we, as Christians are, for this book speaks to our souls, and our souls are made in the images of this book. It stands over against us, outdated, unclear, even faulted with violence invoked against women, yet we are called to listen, for in this book materials for visions are found. Creation with magnificent grandeur, exodus into freedom, singing while in exile, bones dancing, treasures found, sons and daughters speaking, tongues of flame, the city where there is neither tear nor temple: all here is freed for their desires and dreams. The Bible, in the activity of proclamation, refigures time and space in the community. For the Bible ruptures normal linearity in our very reading and hearing of it, as well as by its own words of time. Time and space in the Bible: creation, exodus, flood, exile, prophecy, resurrection, Pentecost, apocalypse. Time and space of otherness, of connectedness, of transformation, of solidarity, of set apartness—the Bible not only speaks about them, but refigures readers/proclaimers in them. The locus of proclamation, at least in this text, is figured through the time and space of God, the Scriptures and community.

The Spirit?

The Spirit of the Lord is upon me,
because he has anointed me to preach good news to the poor.
He has sent me to proclaim release to the captives
and recovering of sight to the blind,
to set at liberty those who are oppressed,
to proclaim the acceptable year of the Lord.

Luke 4:18–19

"The Spirit of the Lord is upon me, because he has anointed me": In one way, the decentered locus of proclamation in God, community, and the Bible already indicates that the process of proclaiming will not be one of God's holy Word poured out upon bent heads or of careful exegesis digging out hidden treasures buried in the text. Rather, the process of proclamation is one which expresses itself only through anointing, "The Spirit of the Lord is upon me," for no matter how careful one's preparation, or loud one's voice, or artistic one's strategy, there remains the claim of anointing in the Spirit.

Biblical scholars debate the role of the Spirit in Luke, they do not dispute that the Spirit is "central."[25] The Spirit appears, for Luke, in ways witnessed to in the Hebrew Scriptures—as wind, breath, prophecy, creativity, force. The Spirit comes to Mary, and the Spirit inaugurates. Yet this does not tell us what the words speak, for it is not enough to explain that, in Luke, the Spirit inaugurates a new age. This text speaks also of God's power and presence, in and through the Spirit that, knowing no boundaries and limits, comes and anoints. The text speaks also of words and community that are received only with the Spirit. The language of the Spirit makes sense, in the horizon of this text, as the language of the margins, a discourse that pushes against the order. By way of contrast, in modern Christianity the Spirit is spoken of in one of two ways: as a psychological aberration or, existentially, as an immediacy of the self to itself. Modernity has tried to "capture" the Spirit, to ban all discourse about the Spirit as God, to again and again relate the Spirit to the needs of the self. Here the Spirit is that which empowers, that which anoints to speech, that which blesses with voice.

This prototype of a discourse of emancipatory transformation puts any discourse about the Spirit on the Spirit's terms, as anointed discourse, that is, in this anointing the Word comes within words. For without the breath and fire of the Spirit, the relation of words and Word is formal and empty, a mathematical equation of the finite and the infinite. It is with the Spirit anointing, the sanctifying of words, that Christianity can turn to speak to the world. As the Scriptures are holy for the ability of their stories to speak the credible claims of freedom, so feminists may proclaim and lay claim to words in Word, only in the Spirit, in the anointing of discourse to bear the responsibility and the gratuitousness of God in the world. In the Spirit words do not make the proclaimer holy, but rather they, through the Spirit, sanctify the world.[26]

The Spirit anoints and blesses words for the world with a purpose; the Spirit cannot be unconnected with God's purpose. The process of proclamation that makes discourse anointed, that makes it full of the Spirit lies here not so much with the speaker, but with the content. It is not enough to define, somewhat formally, the Spirit as the space of God's purpose in anointing Jesus because the anointing is itself direct, and if we, readers/proclaimers, are to receive Jesus and hear the Word as words and words as Word we must receive that to which the Spirit anoints: *he has anointed me to preach good news to the poor. He has sent me to proclaim release to the captives and recovering of sight to the blind, to set at liberty those who are oppressed, to proclaim the acceptable year of the Lord.*

What, then, is the content of this proclamation spoken in the time and space of God, a discourse of the Scriptures, a discourse that speaks in the freedom of God? The third question of proclamation in relation to this text is answered through a vision of the dispossessed and disinherited, of the poor and the blind, of those who live and lose in history. Here the true, good, beautiful, is located: the good news of Jesus anointing to sight, release, hope. That which is rejected in history—indeed, the rejects of history, the "nonpersons," as Gustavo Gutiérrez says—are themselves made into the vision of freedom, of hope, of God.[27]

Luke has, it can be said, a decided preference for the downtrodden, a preference for connecting the poor, the rejected, the outcast with emancipatory transformation.[28] Luke refuses to cooperate with stripping the myths, domesticating the metaphors, reducing the narratives to unnarrated meanings. The vision of God in Luke has to do with the "others" of history; the vision that both guides and is produced in Luke's proclamation of emancipatory transformation is one of being made free, of liberation in actual, factual, historical ways. In this fashion, Luke presents Jesus at the beginning of his ministry announcing, in the community, with the Scriptures, anointed by the Spirit, that he comes to the oppressed.

It is a ministry and a message whose traces travel throughout this text of Luke. Indeed, before Jesus proclaims, it already occurs. The usually silent Mary sings her praise to God for feeding the hungry and sending away the rich. Jesus continues the message with a two-pronged thrust to the rich and the poor; Luke retains the radical connection of Jesus' message to the poor and to the rich: recall, for instance, the terrifying story of Lazarus and the rich man (16:19–26) or the pairing of the beatitudes of blessings with the laments of woe (6:20–26). Who are the poor? Isn't everyone, in some sense, poor? Not so for Luke and for Luke's rendition of Jesus. What do the poor, the blind, and the prisoner have in common with those who hunger, who weep, and who are persecuted and rejected? They live on the margins, they are the neglected—the "others" of human existence, of world, of history. In a more ambiguous manner, Luke emphasizes the position of women. The widow is taken as the one to represent not merely the application of stewardship for churchly pledging, but a model for discipleship. Women, at least on a few occasions, receive God where men do not see; as Eduard Schweizer says,

> Zechariah grows dumb, whereas Elizabeth greets and praises the coming Messiah. Joseph appears merely as an attribute of Mary and has nothing to do with the birth of the Messiah, whereas Mary proves to be the handmaiden of God whom all generations will call blessed. Simeon is ready to depart after his prophecy, whereas Hannah speaks of the Messiah to all who are looking for the redemption of Israel.[29]

To hear this message is to make a twofold acknowledgement: first, to acknowledge Jesus' ministry as focused on the margins in the radical reordering of the present reality, and second, to acknowledge the experience of those on the margins who receive God. Now, living in a time where issues and questions are centered on persons who suffer, this ministry of Jesus is to be received. With the silencing of women, with the battering of women, with the masses of the poor, with the victims of political and psychic violence, this ministry of Jesus stands in stark contrast to the accomplishments of freedom in modernity.

And so the margins receive, not because of the purity of their innocence, not because they are figured as closer to God, but in their openness, their emptiness, their positionality, their fluidity, in which God appears. The margins are emancipated, transformed in their brokenness, their off-centeredness, their hunger to speak of freedom. It is in this fulfillment that visions of emancipatory transformation emerge. In Luke's proclamation, visions of emancipatory transformation speak through the widow who becomes a model for discipleship, the uninvited guests at a banquet, and the woman who could not be distracted into service.[30]

To receive visions of emancipatory transformation in these "others" of history is to re-form and reorder the whole. If one is a woman, to proclaim God's Word is to claim one's voice and power, to be, in this manner, anointed by the Spirit. To receive and to speak is, first, a vision of the nonpersons of history being persons on their own terms. It is, second, to change the reality, the order, the world. Women cannot become men, blacks do not desire to be white, the poor will not be the rich; rather, Luke provokes a vision where difference and specificity can live together with wholeness and connection. The order of life is not dependent on the security of a bourgeois subject, one anthropological construct of "freedom" requiring the unfreedom and oppression of all others. The vision of freedom is a vision of plenitude, a vision of emancipation where all are transformed into freedom, a freedom where all live together. In this text, the content of proclamation is that of emancipatory transformation of all relations, significations, and orders.

Speaking/Hearing

> And he closed the book, and gave it back to the attendant, and sat down and the eyes of all in the synagogue were fixed on him. And he began to say to them: "Today this scripture has been fulfilled in your hearing." (Luke 4: 20–21)

The vision of emancipatory transformation in which reality, history, and human subjectivity are radically changed and reordered, where unity by force gives way to multiplicity by desire and where the freedom of one subject is exploded into the freedoms of many subjects, is no longer just a "vision" as in *visionary* but a vision as in *revision*—to make again, to make now, to be fulfilled. The eschatological longing is present gift. But what can this mean? What is the point of Jesus' own proclamation? Following Jesus' words of Word, what is the point of any proclamation?

This is Luke's first account of Jesus' public ministry, following an explanatory preview. The preview begins with a long genealogy because, in Luke, Jesus is related to the course of history; in the genealogical account Luke establishes not only the radical historical fact of Jesus, but places this in the context of all history.[31] In Jesus, history is not escaped, but made anew, changed, reordered, transformed. The second section on the temptations by Satan in the desert shows Jesus as standing fast because he is armed with the Spirit and the Scriptures. The text before us is Jesus' own declaration, his first act of ministry, the announcement of his mission to preach, to teach, to read words, to heal with the Spirit. To begin this ministry in and of history, Luke selects a particular passage to herald the radical newness in history, and to announce that within its own cries and longings, Jesus begins.

What does it mean that the first account of Jesus' public ministry is the announcement of the fulfillment of this particular text? Does it mean that the text thereby loses all historical importance, or now must be turned into an ethical guide? Or that Jesus declares the desire of his ministry to be to preach the good news of freedom, of celebration, of solidarity? Lucan scholarship steers the reader's questions in a certain way according to Luke's configurations of salvation history. As Fitzmyer has argued in his commentary on Luke, Luke's account is different from other accounts of salvation history, though it is no less valid.[32] Fitzmyer's argument about the theological validity of Luke is important for, until recently, Luke has been neglected and trivialized due to emphasis on eschatology as the center of Jesus traditions, a concern matching the desire for an ahistorical rendition of our own salvation.[33] Likewise, in the midst of the apocalyptic orientation of recent theology, Luke does not lose the vigilance and temporality of the apocalyptic, allowing the apocalyptic its own radical rupture in the life and witness of Christian community. Nor is it fair to discount Luke as a theologian of glory, lacking the strong theology of cross of Paul. Luke cannot be judged against Mark or Paul or John, especially as those books seemingly conform to modern theological standards.[34]

In Luke, Jesus is the herald of the kingdom, appointed not to describe the kingdom or to offer a magical entrance, but to announce its presence as its herald. Jesus establishes the temporal-spatial reality of the kingdom, a reality which the disciples are given the task of realizing.[35] Jesus brings a new era into history, one which affects time and space. Jesus is not "end" or "passage," but the herald, the inauguration, the beginning of the emancipatory reality of salvation for all peoples. The transformative power of the Jubilee images in Luke points to a salvation in which history is not a mere arena of expression or application, but in which history, God, and humanity are configured together.[36] The importance of this passage at the beginning of Jesus' ministry signifies the reordering of the new era, one clearly characterized by salvation as having a time and place in history. Jesus, the herald, announces the message with an explicit content: a kingdom of salvation where relations are reordered.

What does such announcement say about the theological purpose for proclamation? This is not to ask questions about Jesus' understanding of preaching, but more to re-hear what provocation Luke's discourse suggests in relation to the present situation. There is no claim in these pages that Jesus' own understanding can be identified, or if it could that it should be applied in some literal fashion. Rather, in the back and forth movement of the text with us as readers/proclaimers, in the radical otherness of the text that is in front of us, and within our experience as different from the text, we must ask, What do we receive of proclamation? The first clue to answer this question can be borrowed from a claim found in contemporary Lucan scholarship that in Luke there is no great distinction between *kerygma* (preaching) and *didache* (teaching).[37] The proclamation of good news is decidely an event—an event that provokes, changes, converts, turns over, but also one that establishes, reorders, informs, transforms. For Luke's Jesus, the good news is not apart from or beyond history but lived out within and amid history. It is not the case that moral applications may be formed, existential catharsis procured, or presumed identity preserved. The possibility for proclamation is, in Luke's Gospel, itself configured as a way of being Christian, involving the realities in which Christians live. Proclamation is nothing more, and certainly nothing less, than reordering, heralding, reforming. In this view of proclamation, *kerygma* and *didache* are combined, for readers/proclaimers are finally formed and transformed in the pulsation of changing relations. What else is salvation and grace to those on the margins but the reordering of relations? What else is grace but solidarity to live differently? The point of Jesus' proclamation is to announce the fulfillment of new relations, and in this proclamation the disciples find witness to the possibility of new relations. The witnessing is a heralding, not an observation of past events, but a herald of future ways, ways that challenge and change the present. Proclamation is the claiming for now in the present toward the future; it is an anticipatory freedom that proclamation fulfills and sets free.

Is it really so different for Christians now? Is not to render the kingdom in community precisely to realize its disruptiveness that calls into question secured identities, entrenched narratives, self-protected existential beings? Readers/proclaimers are called into question, shaped by new relations, not by a radical call from outside of history, not by a universal moral law within, but in the relations of the social-symbolic order in which we live, by the insurrections of knowledge and practice, the gaps, the releases, the jubilees, that lurk within all relations. Is not the point of women's words of proclamation, in feminist discourses of emancipatory transformation, the fulfillment of the vision, the living/speaking now, the words made flesh and flesh made words of freedom, of healing, of wholeness?

Testimony and Confession

> And all spoke well of him, and wondered at the gracious words which proceeded out of his mouth; and they said, "Is not this Joseph's son?" And he said to them, "Doubtless you will quote to me this proverb, 'Physician, heal yourself; what we have heard you did at Capernaum, do here also in your own country.'" And he said, "Truly, I say to you, no prophet is acceptable in his own country." (Luke 4:22–24)

From the promise of fulfillment, the actual emancipatory transformation in the present that anticipates the future, Luke turns in this text to questions and testimony, providing a space to question how words and life relate in proclamation. This question entails the status of proclamation: how life fits words.

This part of our prototypical text on/of proclamation begins innocently enough, as those who have heard Jesus' proclamation are filled with wonder at his ability to speak such words. Their question seems natural, even complimentary—Is this Joseph's son? Is he not one of us? Do we not know him on our own terms? Is he not representing us with such wonderful words?

Yet, Jesus responds, abruptly, or so it seems, turning their friendly compliments to his paternal heritage into expectations and commands. After announcing the fulfillment of good news to the poor, of liberty to the oppressed, of an acceptable day of transformed relations and restoration anew, Jesus anticipates that his hearers will want him to do what he did in Capernaum. Jesus seemingly opens a space in which, at first glance, we can only assume that Jesus does not want to be known by the name of his father. Is he just a rebellious son who seeks his own identity?

Or is it, this space Jesus opens, more than rebellion, having to do with what it means to be the one proclaiming emancipatory transformation and the need for vigilant resistance to all reduction, not only of life to words but also of words to life. For when emancipatory transformation is reduced to the terms set by the symbolic order, at least in the present situation, the inevitable occurs: the woman who acts like the man, blacks are supposed to be like whites, the poor are simply changed into the rich. Is it not necessary to protect against a reductionism that translates all good news in terms already too familiar and secure?

Let us hear this section, then, as questioning Jesus in relation to his proclamation. For the question of the hearers places Jesus, in a sense, on trial. At least that is how Jesus hears the question, as a trying of his identity. He anticipates where the questioning will lead: a demand for proof upon proof, "Physician, heal yourself; what we have heard you did at Capernaum, do here also in your own country."[38] With their words of wonder and trust, they have placed him on trial, a trial of who is he to proclaim such things. With a quick mastery of words, he constructs the irony: does not the pride of recognition turn to the demand for proof? And proof that will not easily reach satisfaction, for won't one successful proof lead to the need for more proof? By placing him on trial as to his identity through the name of his father, they have misunderstood the vision and its fulfillment, the proclamation of emancipatory transformation.

Once more, Jesus widens the gap between their initial recognition and his response: "No prophet is acceptable in his own country." One proverb, seemingly to answer another: neither of the proverbs are in the community's words; they are, rather, the words of Jesus in response to their recognition, that is, in fact a misrecognition. With this appeal to the prophetic, Jesus allows us to consider proclamation as a testimony to and of God. For the prophetic sense of testimony intensifies proclamation as proceeding, in the words of Paul Ricoeur, from a "divine initiative."[39] Thus proclamation involves our lives and our words as a testimony to what we have seen or heard, or, in the present tense, what we see and hear in relation to ultimate reality.[40] The prophet is not acceptable in his/her own country because of the testimony to God questioning, recreating, renewing, opening, transforming all that has been established as the orderly way.

As a witness to what is seen and heard, testimony involves an act of confession of the self, of who the self is in this act. In this manner the hearers of Jesus are correct to ask who Jesus is. But confession in testimony also points to what has been seen, the narration of action.[41] Thus Jesus' first response, that in their misrecognition of him they will want further proof of his identity, is, at the same time, an accusation that his hearers have refused to hear his testimony as proclamation that narrates the fulfillment of good news to the poor, of release for the prisoner and sight for the blind, of sending the downtrodden away relieved, of proclaiming the time of God's favor. In their misrecognition the hearers have not heard that of which Jesus speaks. In the text before us, proclamation opens out of the testimony of Jesus to the activity of God who calls out and sets free.

But of course confession is also necessary for testimony, since the narration of events occurs within the confession of the testifier.[42] The confession of faith of the testifier is the confession not of one's identity or heritage—not "Joseph's son"—but of one's life, even of the acceptance of suffering and death, martyrdom, for the testimony. Yet even martyrdom, in relation to proclamation, is not itself that which is confessed. That which is confessed, that which martyrdom testifies to, is the vision produced in the fusion of the confession and the narration. Thus we who proclaim, who offer discourses of emancipatory transformation, do so within the involvement of our lives, yes, life unto death if this be the case. But it is not our lives themselves that answer the question of whether we are "Joseph's son"; though proclamation is opened by the confession of our lives, it is the testimony that moves through our desires to narrate freedom in history. Our lives, as Ricoeur suggests, are sealed to these narrated and confessed desires of freedom and not, as Jesus' hearers seemed to suggest, to established terms of the order.[43]

The status of how life relates to words in the proclamation of emancipatory transformation, we might say, is one of openness rather than of closure. In testimony words open up life, life opens up words, but always in relation to the visions produced by the fusion of narration and confession. To put it in terms of the logic of proclamation, the Word as perfectly open sign is testified to in the very act of testimony itself, for in prophetic testimony the open play of confession and narration are productive of aesthetic visions of human flourishing.

Women's lives, in feminist proclamations of emancipatory transformation, are thus sealed to the desires of freedom expressed in the confession and narration of women's testimonies. Women's deeds will not necessarily prove the openness of this freedom, just as the proclaimer cannot guarantee the truth of testimony through satisfying tests of the order. In prophetic discourse, women testify to the openness of their lives, their words, their freedom, thus placing the social-symbolic order on trial by resisting its terms of closure. Women's martyrdom will entail not only the acceptance of death, if that be the case, but, more importantly, the embracement of writing, speaking, and creating life anew in both words and deeds. In this manner proclamation moves through testimony, relying on the power realized in speaking one's own life.

Much more could be said about proclamation as testimony, but at this point it is necessary to note that to testify is always to persuade; testimony is a rhetorical act, an act that moves to judgment. If on one side of proclamation we have testimony, in which the proclaimer's life is sealed to her testimony of freedom, on the other side we have those who hear, who must in turn receive the truth and power of both testimony and proclamation. But at the end of this passage the power and truth of even our testimony in proclamation cannot and will not close the openness of the Word of God.

In the Spaces Between

> But in truth, I tell you there were many widows in Israel in the days of Elijah, when the heaven was shut up three years and six months, when there came a great famine over all the land; and Elijah was sent to none of them but only to Zarephath, in the land of Sidon, to a woman who was a widow. And there were many lepers in Israel in the time of the prophet Elisha; and none of them was cleansed; but only Naaman the Syrian." When they heard this, all in the synagogue were filled with wrath. And they rose up and put him out of the city, and led him to the brow of the hill on which their city was built, that they might throw him down headlong. But passing through the midst of them he went away. (Luke 4:25–30)

This section tempts great puzzlement, though in much biblical scholarship it seems clear enough that Jesus is foretelling the rejection of his mission in his homeland. But there is a movement here that must be questioned, not so much from the perspective of biblical or literary scholarship but in the intertextuality of the Gospel itself, since the configuration of the good news at the end does not at all match the proclamation of the good news at the beginning, even in spite of the scholars' explanation of the rejection of his mission in relation to the fulfillment of his proclamation.[44]

Jesus is one who comes to preach good news to all the oppressed, yet he ends up suggesting that only two are saved. There were, the text says, many widows, but Elijah was sent to only one; there were many lepers, but in the days of Elisha only one was cleansed. Why only one? The furious response by the people suggests that it is not the message of Jesus that is misunderstood. In some way they understood, or thought they understood, this part of the message clearly, perhaps they knew more in their murderous understanding of the words Jesus spoke than in their earlier misrecognition of the identity of Jesus as son of Joseph.[45]

Commentators tend to label this entire passage of Luke a fulfillment-rejection story: "The fulfillment story stresses the success of his teaching under the guidance of the Spirit, but the rejection story symbolizes the opposition that his ministry will evoke among his own."[46] The point seems obviously simple: in the context the narrative moves to demonstrate how Jesus will not really be accepted, a kind of factual expression of what has been noted already in the prophetic testimony of Jesus. Thus, the only widow saved is not an Israelite but a Gentile, and the only leper cleansed is Syrian. The point, according to the commentaries, is obvious: Jesus will not be received by his own people. But there is perhaps another way to read the text, or better yet, to re-hear the text in its own ambiguity, caughtness, rupture. Notice two things: first, the clear disparity in this section between the jubilee image and the prophetic image, and, second, the violence (rather than wonderment) of the community's response.[47]

Beginning then with the interpretation of this text as rejection we can hold this notion of rejection in a relation of conflation to the fulfillment of verses 18–19. To combine the text this way is to transpose the sending of Jesus to the oppressed and the sending of Elijah to the widow Zarephath. Jesus has just finished claiming the reality of God releasing captives, spreading good news, setting at liberty those who suffer oppression—in these words there is no narrowing to a requirement of acceptance. Yes, the widow is not a member of Israel, but the emphasis in this text is not, despite the efforts of interpretation, on her reception but on Elijah's sending. So also with the leper: in verse 18 when miracles are attested to in the recovery of sight to the blind, no mention is made of only one blind person receiving enough to see, but in verse 27, only one leper is cleansed, Naaman the Syrian: the emphasis in this verse is not on the receptivity of Naaman but rather on the figure of Elisha. Displaced here is the vision of new earth, decentered is priestly reordering and prophetic testimony: now there is judgment, rejection, shock.[48]

The text says the people were furious: the worshiping congregation is turned suddenly into a murderous mob. What is going on here, why this reaction that overflows the situation? Surely a rabbi had preached to them before about receptivity! Surely Jesus' questioning of their praise is not enough to lead them to mad fury! Or does the reading of receptivity account for the severity of this text where the congregation is moved from pride to murder in the space of several lines? The text itself provokes the questioning of this as a "rejection" story.

The text forces the reader to pause here, near the endless swirl of freedom, sight, acceptance, testimony, confession, and narration, to consider how it is one "reads" and "hears" this text. Reading, at least in the theories of modern humanistic scholarship, uses the text as a mirror for the subject. This is stated in the extreme by those who, in contemporary church work, speak of finding one's story in the Bible, as if the book is but a mirror, a mirror without flaw, to reflect or represent the image of the already accepted self.

Historical critical methods as a form of scholarship have often been used as technical tools to uncover the meaning of the book; this has already been demonstrated in relation to this text of Luke: historical critical methods explain the text as a fulfillment-rejection story. But does this really get at the voice of the text? How, for instance, would one preach this: that the story is about our rejection, or better yet, that we project into the Bible ourselves as the widow or the leper?[49] It is, in this way, "about" the theme of rejection and thus the subject can be reflected in the text and the text rewritten around the subject. This, of course, presents innumerable problems when it is suggested that the text corrects, challenges, and provokes the reader since the constructs employed by the reader already construe the text as only a mirror.

Historically, the Bible in the church was not a mirror of the self but of God, in the sense of a journey or a path. What was clear for the ancient authors was that the Bible had more than one meaning; indeed, these authors saw any confusion or ambiguity in the text as being placed there by God for religious reasons.[50] Though Protestantism is usually charged with reducing the Bible to the literal meaning, it also tried to protect the plurivocity and the identity of the Bible as the mirror of God through the notions of inner Christ and the Spirit. One could read the Bible and *not* receive the Word, Calvin pointed out, if the Spirit were not present. The Bible, in much of the tradition, is more than the meaning of its words read literally.

Modernity established the limit of the act of reading the Bible to reflect a meaning representative of human existence. It was, of course, a highly ambiguous task for religious scholarship in modernity. On the one hand, scholarship proved that there was no real "book": the Bible was a compilation of different pieces, based on oral history, containing contradictory facts, pieces selected through a process of canonization that was dominated by a political conflict for control of the church. On the other hand, this Book had somehow to be considered a "sacred" text that supported, if not secured, the individual subject, in front of God.[51] The ambiguity was resolved not through biblical scholarship, but through a theological principle in which faith, christologically construed, provides the identity of meaning reflected by the text. Faith, given by the principle of Christ, allows the reception of the text, which in turn reflects the reception of Christ.

Yet neither the importance of biblical scholarship nor the affirmation of a theological principle speaks to the fullness of this passage, for the reader/proclaimer who receives this as proclamation is left with a certain caughtness: a certain image against image, a language against language that no theory of metaphor will solve. What is it finally to have a discourse of solidarity, liberation, and fulfillment, and a discourse of judgment, selection, and rejection passing one another in the same narrative? What is it for the testimony which leads to proclamation suddenly to go in another direction, a direction which unsettles? The passage produces a space between our meaning and proclaiming, it comes in the midst of reading and passes, slips, and breaks away from the reader's own controlling intent. The point to be expressed in the text, if one really believes in that, is not sufficient to speak to what happens in the text: the text clashes against itself, with one who is both fulfillment for us and as one who passes away in the midst of us.

This text suggests to feminist proclamation that proclaimers control neither their own words nor the words of the text. Proclaimers cannot control the reception of their words, thus words of proclamation may be met with violence, despair, uprising, rejection. But this sounds only a "no matter what" over confession and testimony: proclaimer's lives will cling to words of freedom and words of freedom demand the living of one's life, but all may be questioned, rejected, or crucified precisely when the meaning is grasped.

But feminist proclamation is called into question not only by hearers turned violent, but by the text itself. For proclamation, as embodying the Word as open sign, as abductive in the prototype of freedom, must itself be open to multiple meanings in the text and to questions of discomfort and otherness. The Scriptures, precisely as received in a feminist hermeneutics of marginality, can no longer be domesticated as good morals, existential comforts, sweet little narratives. There is now, not only in those who read the Bible but in the reading of the Bible itself, a restlessness of Word and words that moves for emancipatory transformation but that can vanish in the midst of us as proclaimers and as hearers.

And thus the proclamation of emancipatory transformation reaches a fractured resting point. Through a feminist reading of this text, we have attempted to discover the beginnings of a discourse of emancipatory transformation in the text of Luke. Yet near the end of proclamation and testimony, the text questioned the discourse and shied away from the testimony. The text became broken, the margins shielded multiple meanings, and the question of who one is in reading and proclaiming this story remains open. The testimony of one's life, as reader and proclaimer, must cling to words of freedom, but freedom itself will not be controlled by one's words.

Reordering Our Relations

Luke has been read through a feminist hermeneutics of marginality as a prototype of proclamation in the Word as open sign. From this reading two focuses express themselves as further developments of proclaiming the Word to and for the world in the present situation. The first focus concerns proclamation as discourses constitutive of community, wherein the Christian community is constituted through the discursive practices of its proclamation. The second focus concerns proclamation as discourses of reordering relations in the social-symbolic order, relations not only of men and women but also of time and space, of poor and rich, of human subjectivity, of reading, of healing. In this reading, proclamation has been constitutive both of Christian community and of Christian life in witness and confession, but it is proclamation only when it is lived to and for the reordering of relations in the world. Thus proclamation constitutes the church; it is who the church is and what the church does. Though it is undeniably necessary in the logic of proclamation to consider in what manner proclamation constitutes the community in order to speak to the world, in order of purpose, the second focus of proclamation receives the priority and thus requires the initial comment.

It is perhaps the stirring words of Isaiah, cast now in the fulfillment of the herald, that first moves the reader/proclaimer in this passage. Words that suggest no easy solution to suffering, oppression, guilt, and injustice. Rather, the jubilee is invoked, a jubilee which is now removed from the priestly injunction of respite and is transformed into the mission and message of Jesus as the inauguration of a new era in history.[52] Here, proclamation becomes the discourse of this reordering of relations, a discourse that both frees and transforms, a discourse that speaks in and for new relations, new fulfillments, new forms of being. In such a manner, through a feminist hermeneutics of marginality, Luke's proclamation has been received as one model for feminist discourse and as a prototype for what feminist proclamation is to be.

Proclamation, in its broadest sense, encompasses the discourses of emancipatory transformation of Christian community to and for the world. Such is the role, nature, and mission of Christianity, to provide Word and words of emancipatory transformation, discourses that criticize and transform the established relations of sin, oppression, distortion, and suffering. In this manner, proclamation is extended beyond its modern sense of helpful information to Christian gentlepersons or the announcement of good news to the already saved.[53] Rather, proclamation is the entirety of the discourses that Christianity gives to the world including the naming of sin, critiques of ideology, images of human flourishing, blessings of grace, songs of hope, and praises to God. Proclamation, and thus Christianity, is given to and for the world.

In the present situation, proclamation seeks to address not only specific issues of the day—issues of injustice, of environmental destruction, of nuclear annihilation—but also the relations, orders, and rules that create those situations. Thus, proclamation must address not only specific situations in which women are oppressed or excluded, but also the system itself, the rules that allow oppression to be expressed in thousands of ways, the principles that make the oppression a systemic distortion and not just individual acts of ill intent; rules that, as shall be examined, create subjectivity as individual identity through the constant division of man and woman, that make language always represent the intention of speaker or writer, that form politics as self-preservation. Principles that necessitate space be always "controlled" rather than dwelled in and adorned; that time be linear or existential rather than cyclical or cosmic. Such rules and principles are today the deepest values, orderings, and metaphors that constitute the barriers to freedom. This is why the space and time of the proclamation in Luke is so striking, because proclamation begins in its locus in God's space and time, a space and time that is today marginal to the space and time of modernity, and in its marginality both critical and transformative of the ordering. It is also why, in Luke, it is important to ask how reading occurs, and how, despite the fragmentariness of the text, the modern way of reading wants to project the concluding section of the Lucan text as a mirror to existential rejection.

Proclamation, in feminist discourses of emancipatory transformation, resists and transforms the social-symbolic order. Proclamation is a form of resistance to the practices and principles of modernity that control, dominate, and oppress. But proclamation resists by way of transformation, seeking to provide new discourses by a variety of strategies, methods, and ways, and to transform the ruling principles and order into ones that allow, encourage, and enable transformative relations of multiplicity, difference, solidarity, anticipation, embodiment, and transformation. Transformation occurs by creating new images of human flourishing, new values of otherness and multiplicity, new rhetorical practices of solidarity and anticipation.

Through discourses of emancipatory transformation, proclamation enables those marginalized voices who so often have not been heard, to speak: to speak of the beauty, hope, pain, and sorrow they have known on the margins. Proclamation also speaks within the ambiguities of the order, the ambiguities, for instance, of the bourgeois who, though promised freedom in his autonomy, discovers few genuine possibilities for the community, relationships, and love he so desires. Unable to find any "authentic meaning" the bourgeois attempts to fill in the empty spaces of his or her desire through the attainment of material goods that grant momentary satisfaction with increasingly diminished returns.[54] Resistance and transformation occur, then, through the lacing, locking, and jamming of the ambiguities of the order and the border of its chaos. The ambiguity and distortion of bourgeois desire become the stuff of proclamation joining the voices of those long silenced to find new ways to speak of freedom.

Such a task, the task of resisting and transforming modernity through discourses of emancipatory transformation, leads back to a reconsideration of the first focus, proclamation as constitutive of community. To form Christianity as a proclamation of this Word and words of resistance and transformation, as discourses that suggest new ways to speak of freedom and new attitudes and practices of being human, requires an emancipatory transformation of Christianity. The Christianity of feminism, which today promotes such discourse, is marginal, fragmentary, barely able to be glimpsed in the situation in which I live. Yet it is present: in relationships, in books and poems, in stories from other places, in small gatherings, in prayers of freedom. To offer discourses of freedom to the world, discourses that will be heard not merely in isolated cases or separate minority reports, Christianity will have to be reformed, shaped anew out of its dreams and stories, its present experiences, its hopes for future.

To find new ways of speaking, it will be necessary to oppose old and comfortable habits, habits that in the present forms of modern Christianity secure the individual existentially, while dividing the subject materialistically as guarantor of the public and private.[55] The discourse of Christianity in modernity became primarily a discourse of individual subjectivity that, at its worst, threatened to secure middle-class existence as essentially good, while, at the same time, serving as a discourse to smooth over the limits beyond that existence, limits confronted in death, illness, and despair. This served to render the church as a "protective" institution whose role it is to serve as a space for individual expression and development while maintaining its own institutional status.

Despite the pluralism within modern Christianity, there is, nonetheless, a fundamental accommodation of modern Christianity, as seen from the marginality of feminist discourse, to the social-symbolic order. Indeed, many of the Christian discourses that seem to oppose specific facets of modern culture still accept its basic terms and rules, such as the structure of human existence, the autonomy of the individual, history as progress. This pact of accommodation must be questioned in Christian proclamation precisely as proclamation—through emancipatory transformation—is constitutive of Christian community. But such questioning must occur only as Christianity itself experiences the good news of emancipatory transformation, only as Christianity itself is transformed in and through the proclamation of Word to and for the world.

It is, then, as Luke suggests, the peculiar activity of testimony and confession that Christian community enables in feminist proclamation. For, constituted in and through God's time and space, in Word embodied in the words of women, it is possible to speak of the trial of the world. In giving testimony, feminists narrate the credible claims of freedom: stories of Scripture, promises of hope, prayers of petition, bonds of solidarity. Confession is not for the sake of the order; it is not to let women in or to make women into men, nor to give women patriarchal powers. Rather, confession is for the testimony of this freedom: of reordered relations where women and men are not contained through binary oppositions, where otherness and multiplicity are enjoyed with blessings of grace.

If this reading of Luke is at least provocatively a prototype, then proclamation today begins in the caughtness of fulfillment and rejection, in solidarity with the margins but in the openness of what emancipatory transformation may mean. But in this caughtness, it is necessary not to be disuaded by the difficulties of proclamation. The logic of proclamation, as developed thus far, leads us to consider the nature of Christian community, both through the experiences of women and through the ambiguities in representative discourses of modern Christianity. But to follow the logic of proclamation in this fashion is to hope for anointed speech, that such talk of community will occur because of the purpose and task in which feminism proclaims the Word as perfectly open sign. This is the task that the Spirit guides: to make community constituted in God's time and space that today finds new ways to speak of freedom and finds anew ways of speaking freely. Between fulfillment and rejection, it is possible to ask, Can the Christian community speak again the Word to the world, not the Word of the world, but the Word that opens up good news to all, that in the feminist voices of emancipatory transformation proclaims release to the prisoners and sight for the blind, sets at liberty those oppressed, and proclaims the Lord's year of favor?

·3·

THE COMMUNITY OF EMANCIPATORY TRANSFORMATION

. . . what is implied is that language, and thus sociability, are defined by boundaries admitting of upheaval, dissolution, and transformation. Situating our discourse near such boundaries might enable us to endow it with a current ethical impact. In short, the ethics of a linguistic discourse may be gauged in proportion to the poetry that it presupposes.

Julia Kristeva

God is a God of freedom. From creation to exodus to exile to Christ to church, the Bible explores this fact: the call of freedom, the claim of freedom, the lusty desire of freedom. The Bible narrates, in spite of its own hierarchical madness, despite any attempts to tame it, that freedom is the gift of both creation and redemption. People read the Bible, and the Bible reveals the longing for peace, the reign of a pure city, the celebration of dancing bones, the cleansing healing of anger expressed. There are, of course, other issues, things, images in the Bible, and at times they speak in voices other than that of freedom; at times they even speak to silence freedom. But yet, in some way or another, freedom speaks.

In our own time and space, when life itself grasps for its survival and for life anew, when the social-symbolic order so desperately needs emancipation and transformation, when systemic violence and psychic destructiveness together allow no place for us to flourish, the Bible speaks of freedom in the words of emancipatory transformation: emancipatory to heal the wounds of human destructiveness, to celebrate differences and particularities, to give life anew; transformative to change the present systems of hierarchy and madness, to discover new possibilities of justice and to create new forms of flourishing. The Bible provokes, envisions, discloses, offers, and describes emancipatory transformation for all.

Yet this horizon of freedom is not just somehow "there," it is not a secret message in the text open to a selected few. According to the logic of proclamation in the last chapter, the horizon of freedom in the Bible is not finally a textual horizon, something that, on a given day, can be picked up, analyzed, and reproduced. For this horizon of freedom is alive, is provoked, is disclosed, is offered in the embodied relations of Word and words called the church. As Christianity offers discourses of emancipatory transformation to and for the world, the church must be the embodiment of emancipatory transformation, that which constitutes the proclamation and that from which this proclamation comes. The church must be the freedom of the embodied Word, embodied in glimpses of hope that the Bible gives, embodied in Word as perfectly open sign, embodied in human action and contemplation.

Is this not the vision of Luke's proclamation: the community who gathers in God's time and space—time of fullness, connection, and rupture, in spaces of solidarity, intersubjectivity, and possibility? As the community which receives the fulfillment of good news, the church is the scene of emancipatory transformation: relations reordered, the church is the community whose texture is made, sustained, and constantly renewed through discourses of freedom. By being a space and time of freedom the church proclaims emancipatory transformation, discovering and creating new ways of speaking freely. The church proclaims emancipatory transformation and the church lives in and through this proclamation of emancipatory transformation.

The reconstruction of proclamation in this chapter begins with the exploration of present ecclesial spaces where emancipatory transformation takes place. This chapter attends to the spaces of women-church, for in these marginal and even fragmentary places is the promise of what Christianity, thus far, has repressed and denied: the church as embodied relations of emancipatory transformation depends not upon placing women on the margins, but on being a gathered assembly which lives through nurturing and celebrating values of difference, specificity, embodiment, solidarity, anticipation, and transformation.

Standing in these spaces, with visions of women-church, it is possible to analyze the modern church by examining how the church is regarded by its political radicals, its moderate critics, and its hungering participants. In this analysis, an unfulfilled desire appears: a desire for community, connections, and embodied relations of Word and words in life together. This desire for community also appears, theologically speaking, in two of the most well-known modern theologians, Friedrich Schleiermacher and Karl Barth, in their insistence on community as the nature of the church. An analysis of Schleiermacher and Barth provides not only the ambiguity which may be probed to rend and renew the modern church, but also the steps through which such theological reconstruction is to be developed.

By weaving together the ambiguity of desire for community in modern theology and the Word as open sign and the marginality of women-church, it is possible to reconstruct the church as the community of emancipatory transformation in three steps. The first step calls for a new poetics of community in the proclamation of emancipatory transformation. No longer funded on the unique Word of God apart from history, the church, as women-church, must be funded through a poetics that nourishes community in the constant play of images, in an ongoing communion of words and Word. In this new poetics, the church becomes implicitly a community of poets, a worshiping community, that finds new ways to discover and create the beauty and flourishing of life in Word and words.

After developing the possibility of funding a new poetics of community, the relations of life together requires credible formulation in the proclamation of emancipatory transformation. In this second step, the modern church as the cult of individuals and the cult of institutions is replaced by the intersubjectivity of community in women-church. This intersubjectivity of life together in emancipatory transformation leads to the formulation of the church as a community of rhetoric by foregrounding the dialogical nature of life together. Considering the church as a community of rhetoric emphasizes the intersubjectivity, the situationality, and the transforming nature of life together, but rhetoric itself is a term with a history that must be reformulated away from the freedom of propertied citizens to the freedom represented in women-church, the freedom of all those created and redeemed, past, present, and future. The rhetoric of community suggests that life together is neither closed nor defined by identity and autonomy, but is open and is constituted by difference and connection and lived in solidarity with the world.

The poetics and rhetorics of community lead, in the third step, to a reconstruction of Christian piety. This piety, only intimated in this chapter, is characterized by the gifts of justice and vitality, as well as by the gifts of wisdom and love. With these gifts the church may become, in the logic of proclamation, the embodiment of the Word to and for the world by forming itself through its discourses of emancipatory transformation.

The Margins of Women-Church

Are there anywhere signs of community, connection, relationships, and emancipatory transformation in and of the church? Is the good news of reordered relations, of the lame being healed, of the blind given sight, of the poor lifted up, of the oppressed being freed, given testimony to in ways of life and words of freedom? If community is where time and space are set free by God, where the words of plenitude flow freely, where the testimony of life is sealed to the discourse of freedom, then where today does such community exist? For only if the Word, the Scriptures, and women's dreams and desires speak through a locus of realized freedom can feminism rend and renew the church in the proclamation of emancipatory transformation.

The possibility of speaking of freedom, of proclaiming emancipatory transformation, resides in the reality that at the margins of modern Christianity there are communities that already proclaim emancipatory transformation. The black church, composed of many voices, goals, and liturgies, speaks today the Word in words that rend and renew, that liberate and transform, that heal distraught identities and transform lives into good news.[1] The ecclesial movement in Latin America called basic Christian communities exists within and outside of the official "ecclesial" organization to empower the poor into the feast of Christian fellowship.[2] Even within the modern church in the first world, are churches that struggle to witness, to pray, to act together not as one more form of what Johannes Baptist Metz calls bourgeois religion but as messianic communities.[3]

There is, as well, the reality of women in the church, the possibilities of women-church, the dream of women for a church that is equal and that includes women, recognizes their voices, heals their pain, and celebrates their desires.[4] This dream is present in words of the Scriptures, in words not yet received in the history of scriptural interpretation, words of women as disciples, words of households of inclusivity, of women as ecclesial leaders, of women as voices of freedom. Among the practices of women through history and now, this dream still lives in women working together, in women's mission societies, in women's Bible studies, wherever women are gathered. In these relationships of strength and beauty women are religious, bonded together in Word and words. In washing the dishes after a church supper, in communities of service for women only, in groups that pray and share their women's lives, in mourning the losses of the community, women share together the good news of emancipatory transformation.

This sharing together in emancipatory transformation, however, is partial at present. The vision of women-church, a church not only inclusive of women but embodying relations of emancipatory transformation for all, is based on the fragmentary and partial realization of women's bonding. Women's bonding, that which has often filled the pews, taught the children, baked the bread, done the dishes, and sewed the quilts has not been the central order of the church. The church, as officially established, is run by men, founded on the unique Word of God, and maintained through hierarchical relations of power, knowledge, and interest. In the margins, the margins which have in fact been the precondition for this order, women have worshiped, prayed, sung, taught, listened, worked, hoped, dreamed, loved.

With the advent of feminist theology, women came to question, with loud voices, their role in the church. At first women's only plea to the church was to be let in, to have access to the Word and to represent that Word they had so long been denied. Many churches identified with the Protestant tradition (having no official discourse of women such as that of the Virgin Mary and very few "organized" religious communities of women) allowed women access to the Word by ordination and opened up leadership roles to women. Other churches, including the Roman Catholic church, continued the traditional ordering in more explicit fashion, protecting the Word from direct access to women by claiming to protect the full dignity of women by securing complimentary roles in which men always happen to have the higher position.[5]

Some women saw that moves to equality were moves to further the identity of Word and order, to make women be like men in the religious ordering. These women separated themselves from Christianity and developed new ways of religion, ethics, life, and love. Separatism was born with visions of goddesses, witches, and "thealogy." Yet this changes neither the order nor recognizes seriously enough the power of the order to allow a few separate spaces so dominance can be maintained. Though these moves celebrate the strength of women's power and the possibility of alternative visions, they far too often do not question the depth of the connection between the order and its margins, and do not see that their separatism functions in one more fashion to serve the needs of the order.

The relation of women and the church is as painful and difficult as that of women and the Word, since the Word configured as the unique foundation of the church demands women's marginality. For many years feminists in the church were divided among the so-called reformists, who stayed within the church to get women in, and the so-called radicals, who left to form new ways of being religious.[6] In the present situation, however, a new movement among women is occurring, a movement not merely to correct the ecclesial ordering, but a movement to rend and renew the church as religious community, to resist the present order and to transform not only the application of the rules, but the rules, visions, categories, and relations of the *ecclesia*. Indeed, the most visionary force in feminist theology is found among the writings of women on the church. After years of criticism, negotiating, playing with the rules, wearing men's vestments and speaking in men's voices, women-church, the visionary movement of a new *ecclesia*, prepares now to rend and renew the church.[7] Women-church is not for women only, but for women and men who, now, in restlessness and hope, hear the Word, receive the vision, and speak together words of emancipatory transformation. Women-church is the questioning of new possibilities, the experimentation with new forms, the envisioning of new relations. Seen through the terms of difference, specificity, embodiment, solidarity, anticipation, and transformation, what is *ecclesia*? What happens when the church experiments with models of community rather than securing structures of bureaucracy? What occurs when the church is the embodiment of emancipatory transformation in its life together and in its mission rather than the instantiation of private religious experience and occasional acts of charity? With these questions and others, women-church announces its reality and vision.

Women-church, as envisioned by Rosemary Radford Ruether, relocates the reality of church among women in opposition to naming present ecclesiastical structures as church. For Ruether, women-church is an exodus church:

> As Women-Church we claim the authentic mission of Christ, the true mission of Church, the real agenda of our Mother-Father God who comes to restore and not to destroy our humanity, who comes to ransom the captives and to reclaim the earth as our Promised Land. We are not in exile, but the Church is in exodus with us. God's Shekinah, Holy Wisdom, The Mother-face of God has fled from the high thrones of patriarchy and has gone into exodus with us.[8]

For Ruether the image of the exodus church underscores the liberating reality of women-church, because in this ecclesial reality that exists within the established church and in related organizations, there is the liberating activity of God and the persons who have been liberated from oppression to fulfill the visions of freedom. Exodus suggests, in Ruether's prophetic-iconoclastic approach, the destructiveness and distortedness of the institutional church: as Ruether says, "They have become all too often occasions of sin rather than redemption, places where we leave angry and frustrated rather than enlightened and healed."[9]

Elisabeth Schüssler Fiorenza uses the image the "ekklesia of women" to name the movement of women-church.[10] "Ekklesia" means "the assembled gathering of free citizens to determine their affairs," suggesting the future hope that the church will embody the emancipatory transformation of all persons determining together their Christian praxis. The "ekklesia of women" suggests the self-determination of women, their commitment, accountability, and solidarity. Yet this future hope is based in Christian reality, the reality of baptism, the reality of women's community, the vision of the Gospels in "the communal proclamation of the life-giving power of the Spirit-Sophia and of God's vision of an alternative community and world."[11] From our present reality we draw the future vision, the vision of the full people of God, existing in mutual relations, determining together their ongoing Christian praxis.

For both authors, women-church signifies the rending and renewal of the present ecclesial reality. Elisabeth Schüssler Fiorenza invokes the "ekklesia of women" to underscore the self-determination of women, the need to break the mediation of relationships of women and God through men and to proclaim the freedom of women to claim the power of their heritage, and to affirm women and women's body as the model of the church. Ruether's naming of women-church through the imagery of exodus speaks to the needs and desires of women in the present situation who are creating new liturgies for healing, speaking, celebrating, and connecting anew with God, earth, and one another. Women-church functions as an embodied principle of spiritual community: it is wherever persons participate in and are transformed by the divine.[12] It may be found in organized churches, it may be formed in communities, it flourishes wherever two or three women are gathered in the Spirit, it is wherever women and men are set free to proclaim emancipatory transformation.

Yet the reality and vision of feminist ecclesiology calls for more than the invocation of women-church in the desperate desire to claim a space for women that retrieves their heritage and restores their bodies. The exodus image, the image of freedom, is also the image that represents the creation of religious community through the separation of women and the Word. The church continues this separation of women and the Word through principles of ordering the Word itself as apart from the body, the difference, the specificity represented by women. The "ekklesia of women," as Elisabeth Schüssler Fiorenza realizes, is but a vision today, for women cannot determine their praxis until they transform the church, its meaning, its structures, and its language, by discourses of emancipatory transformation. As women and the Word have bonded together—and as, in this new connection, the biblical words of emancipatory transformation are heard into speech—so must community be envisioned anew: set free from its modern limits, born in the desire of people's lives, created in the Word that gives, restores, and transforms all life. Community must be nurtured in the new relations of emancipatory transformation. Only when the Word as perfectly open sign works through women's words to claim new forms of communion will women-church be more than a dream born out of a marginal, fragmentary reality. For the church must be the embodied reality of the Word of God in the proclamation of emancipatory transformation—a community that speaks of freedom and experiences, together, the freedom of speaking.

The Modern Church

The possibility of women-church as the good news of emancipatory transformation for the church depends in part upon finding places in the modern church that are open for transformation. It is important to begin with a careful analysis of the reality of the church in modern culture, asking what the church is and what it is for, as well as the possibilities for rending and renewing the church as the community of proclamation of emancipatory transformation. If today new ways of speaking of freedom and new freedom to speak must be discovered, then it is necessary to find new places, organizations, and relations in which to learn to speak and from which to speak to the world. Such relations must nurture new discourses of freedom with visions of restoration, with the reality of reordered relations, with possibilities for human flourishing. Since there is no way to start over, and separatism is both impossible and unethical, feminism must pursue the transformation of the church as a place where, with Bible and Word, Christians can learn, through speaking words of emancipatory transformation, to live together in freedom, in celebration, in hope.

Chapter 1 considered the ordering of modern Christianity in the hermeneutical practices of reading the Scriptures through theological principles adopted in the modern contract between a universal structure of human existence and Christian theological anthropology. In modernity, the locus of Christianity has been the individual man, the bond of Christianity between God and man secured in a universal structure of human existence. Because the locus of Christianity is both ahistorical and individualistic, the church has not been realized as in any way constitutive for Christian life, though it has functioned as a place to express, develop, and share one's individual Christian growth and development. In modernity, Christians may attend a church to nurture their Christianity (or to have children nurtured), to join collectively with other Christians to express faith (in ways acceptable to all), or to act out certain Christian commitments (since gathered communities usually can accomplish more than individuals). In many forms of Christian education, Christians have learned to use the Bible to identify mirror images of their struggles, since the principles employed to read the Bible require that it reflect or mirror the meaning of the individual. Modern Christians have heard, on a weekly basis, a sermon, the sole meaning of proclamation in the modern church, addressed to the individuals collected together for moral-religious instruction, existential catharsis, or the narrative location of one's journey.

Criticism of the modern church arises from a variety of places today. Women increasingly find that the modern church does not and will not support their questions, visions, and voices.[13] Moderate cultural critics accuse the modern church of failing to nurture and nourish the remnants of religious virtues and civil responsibilities.[14] Church leaders worry over shrinking membership and the growing apathy, asking, "Are we yet alive?"[15] Church members complain about the lack of leadership in the clergy and the lack of nourishment in church programs. As the proclamation of emancipatory transformation in Luke questions the accommodation of modern Christianity to culture, so do the needs of persons question the complacency with which modern Christianity has accepted its role.

Jürgen Moltmann in his well-known *Theology of Hope* has offered one of the most trenchant criticisms of the modern church. Moltmann begins his analysis by locating the modern church in the change in the church's role in society from *cultus publicus* to *cultus privatus.*[16] Before modernity, Moltmann contends, the Christian faith served as the religious center of society. Modernity formed itself in part by emancipating itself from this center: rather than society serving God, in modernity society serves the needs of the individual.[17] As *cultus privatus* the church serves three roles in modernity: (1) it is the cult of subjectivity, where private matters are dealt with upon individual, existential levels; (2) it is a Noah's Ark fellowship, where lonely individuals come for community, a community that maintains its superficiality through its basic existence as a collection of individuals; and (3) it is an institution that maintains itself like any other institution in the modern world, through practices of business management and bureaucracy.[18]

In the first and third roles, those having to do with individual needs and corporate institutions, the modern church has met its greatest success by serving what more moderate critics would call the therapeutic and managerial functions of modern society. Moltmann analyzes the first role of the modern church by considering the alienating character of modernity's organization of work and service wherein "man" saves himself through a transcendental subjectivity, separating himself constantly from that which he owns, produces, and services, and from the technical and physical world.[19] Christianity locates itself within this transcendental subjectivity, securing absoluteness away from the social and material factors of modernity. In this manner, the modern church tries to be a place for the individual to meet his needs, to assert his Christian ethics of individual responsibility, and to be a totally modern person.

Abiding by the rules of the modern order, the third function of the modern church fills the roles and procedures of modern rationality in the cult of the institution. The private individual, secure in the absolute of the unconditional in the conditional, fits easily the institutionalization of the social order. As Max Weber realized, bureaucracies express not only modern rationality but modern power, for instrumental calculation objectifies all relations into means and ends, benefits and utility.[20] There is little debate in the modern church about its theological purposes or nature, for its clients vote with their feet based on their individual opinions while its bureaucrats pursue technical strategies for growth and development. Thus, as one ecclesial leader was prone to repeat, "The bottom line is that if we ordain women, we will see a decline in church membership." In modernity, the church and theology are, through the cult of the institution, supposedly entirely separate from each other, though it is, of course, through the managerial model that they reflect the same view: the public world of society and the private world of meaning do not meet, for any possible encounter is displaced through the mediating bureaucratization of the modern church.

Yet between the cult of subjectivity and the cult of the institution may be found, even if it is somewhat against Moltmann's analysis, the possibility of pursuing the formulation of the church as community. In Moltmann's second function of the modern church as the cult of fellowship, a desire appears for community, for fellowship, perhaps, even, for solidarity. Moltmann, loyal to his own method of a dialectics of contradiction, fails to see the possibility of transformation in this desire of the bourgeoise for community.[21] Caught between individualism on the one side, and bureaucracy on the other, many seek community, a commonness, a meeting, a recognition of the intersubjectivity of life. Yet, given the basic ordering of a self-reflective Word founding religious collectivism, the modern congregation must form its community by trying to appease individual differences, promoting, at most, a common belief or common perspective held by all individuals. This places a tremendous burden on the congregation (and its "official" minister) to be pleasing to all people, to mold itself into a homogeneous whole, to find its fellowship in a group of people that, at least on the surface, are similar, and value each other for their shared opinions, beliefs, and interests. This results, as Moltmann suggests, in a community that exists like a Noah's Ark, a fragile ark in the flood of hopelessness.[22] It neither questions the relation of Word and community, nor does it share Word with world; this community struggles to hold itself together through the flood of despair and hopelessness.

It is in this second role, the role of the church as providing community, that a place appears for the theologically reconstruction of proclamation and community in the rending and the renewal of the church. For the desire of community, as a substantive entity which constitutes faith, stands in contrast to the individualization of faith and the bureaucratization of ecclesial structures. Despite Moltmann's critical reading of community, the desire for community stands in opposition to the ordering of modernity that he so masterfully discloses. For in this desire, even when the desire is met by creating islands in which "man" can endure his existence, lies the possibility of theologically reconstructing a community that can proclaim emancipatory transformation. Indeed this desire, bequeathed to us in modern theology, provides us with steps to rend and renew the Christian community through women-church and the Word as perfectly open sign.

Many modern theologians, long advocates of relations between the individual and God, insist on community as the mediating link of Word, Scripture, and faith. Indeed, on this issue, there is a great similarity between two otherwise often opposed theologians, Freidrich Schleiermacher and Karl Barth, both of whom preferred to speak of the church as community.[23] Though often overlooked by later readers, both of these great figures of modern theology claimed that *community* names not only the nature of the church but also the location of the *kerygma*—the proclamation of the good news. For Schleiermacher (especially in *Glaubenslebre*), community was both the vehicle of religious consciousness and the goal of all religious consciousness; for Schleiermacher Christian piety could live only in the corporate life of the Christian community.[24] Indeed, Schleiermacher went so far as to argue that the Holy Spirit comes to the community, "the Holy Spirit is the union of the divine Essence with human nature in the form of the common Spirit animating the life in common believers."[25]

Barth, who placed a bust of Schleiermacher in the center of his study (to keep before his eyes the one whom he considered the most formidable exponent of "modern theology"), expresses agreement, at least in principle, on the issue of community. Barth, of course, opposed Schleiermacher's turn to experience with a methodological principle of the Word as Wholly Other, but turned, interestingly enough, to community as the place of the Word. Indeed, Word creates community and community witnesses to the Word. "The community is confronted and created by the Word of God. It is *communio sanctorum,* the communion of saints, because it is *congregatio fidelium,* the gathering of the faithful. As such, it is the *coniuratio testium,* the confederation of the witnesses who may and must speak because they believe."[26] Undeniably, the poetic image of the community as built on the Word is different than that of being the womb of piety, but also undeniably, Schleiermacher and Barth agree on the centrality of community for Christian life.

We must underscore that Schleiermacher and Barth are asking different questions with different desires for religious piety, questions and desires that result in different problems in each theologian's writings. Schleiermacher asked about the presence of God and ended up elevating individual religious experience; Barth asked about the otherness of God, and ended up reifying God and God's Word. But they both began, no matter how problematically, with the questions of the world, of the Bible, of the community of freedom. Schleiermacher spoke to a world breaking into the "freedom" of modernity, a freedom centering in the "I" of individual self-consciousness. To speak was for Schleiermacher to find God in the consciousness of the one who says "I," and thus to find the grounds of freedom that are different from this I. But because this I seemed increasingly to subordinate God to its experience, the history of the I became demonic. In the ruins of the culture of the autonomous I, Barth hammered out the words of freedom apart from history in the majesty of the Wholly Other. The key from Schleiermacher and Barth is not to reprise their voices, for these theologians no longer live with the present questions, but to follow a suggestion by them about community and Word as prior to the individual that they themselves felt tempted to ignore systematically and substantively in their theologies.

A leverage can be gained for theological reconstruction by reconsidering Schleiermacher and Barth in relation to women-church and the Word as perfectly open sign. For Barth and Schleiermacher provide the necessary steps in a theological reconstruction of community by suggesting a process of rethinking community in its relation to Word, in its corporate life together and in its piety.[27] First, using Barth it is possible to formulate the basis of community in relation to the Word through the poetics of community. Second, in relation to both Barth and Schleiermacher the corporate nature, or life together, of community can be constructed through the rhetorical practices of community. And third, following Schleiermacher, the piety of community can be identified through considering the gifts of the Spirit. Though Barth and Schleiermacher provide one possibility of transformation in modern Christianity, it is necessary to state emphatically that both Schleiermacher and Barth failed to reconsider the underlying relation of Word, women, and community and thus both had to define and constitute Christian community only in relation to the dominant social-symbolic order. Schleiermacher correlated the Word with rules of the order, Barth attempted to counterpose those rules unto the Word, but both accepted the finality of the rules themselves. In this fashion, the Word could only accept or negate the world; it was not the Word as perfectly open sign that could fund words of emancipatory transformation.

The feminist task is to reconstruct the relation of the Word as perfectly open sign and the community of emancipatory transformation in the logic of proclamation. The Word emerges through the words of women as the perfectly open sign blessing difference, specificity, embodiment, solidarity, transformation, and anticipation. Recast, restored, and rewoven, this Word today is embodied in the community that proclaims emancipatory transformation. Feminism's theological reconstruction of Christian community can begin with Barth by asking how, within the words of women, community is created in, with, and through the Word in the reception of the Scriptures and the reality of emancipatory transformation.

The Poetics of Community

Though feminist theology expresses the desire and necessity for reformulating the church as community, the difficulties of conceiving and nurturing community are manifest. The modern world provides little structural or symbolic support for substantive community and Christian tradition has celebrated, time and time again, a "community" that is not communal for all persons, not connected to nature, and not fully historical. To take on this enormous task it is necessary to create, theologically, a relation of community to the Word that is truly communal and open, and to provide symbols and images of community that can fund and nurture the difficult task of creating community in today's world. Barth's insistence that community is confronted and created by the Word, is one place to begin, by asking, how, given the Word as perfectly open sign in feminism's theological semiotics and pragmatics, it is possible to name—through a profusion of new images, metaphors, songs, and visions—the relation of Word and community. Such naming—which I shall call a new poetics—is necessary not only to recognize the relation of Word and community, but also to fund and nurture the basic images of community. These, in turn, establish and sustain the relations of community.

To name a new relation of Word and community is today a necessity in the church and in the world. In the church, this relation must be received anew to live again in emancipatory transformation, to be set aflame with the Spirit of power and love, to connect again community and God. For a world that has distorted the richness of difference and particularity into the violence of control and repression and that suffocates the plenitude of desires and dreams, the possibilities of community today must be heard and lived out. Because of the intense desire for community and because of the lack of ways, words, and images for creating community, feminist theology forms a new poetics of the church. By a poetics I mean not a mere continuation of older images, ways of speaking, or metaphors for community, but new forms, pictures, images, and sounds of community. Poetics pushes the limits, plays with the boundaries, and allows participation in communion with the Word. A poetics of community will not replace other modes of discourses in community, but it will fund their richness and fullness in a communion of words which is multivocal and multiform, dense and rich, imagistic and creative.[28] Such a poetics that allows community to be communion with Word is itself a process of emancipatory transformation that informs and reforms all our other modes of discourse.

To formulate Christian community feminist theology begins, as did Barth, with a poetics that funds images of how community is formed in the Word.[29] From visions in the Bible to fragmentary realities in our lives, the Word empowers the community called church: it creates, bonds together, forms the corporate nature. Likewise the community is the manifestation of Word for the world, as the community that is created in emancipatory transformation and as the community that proclaims emancipatory transformation in the world. In feminism's poetics of community, there must be no illusion that the Word somehow founds community apart from the richness of the body of human existence; nor any deceit that the words and discourses of community are merely empty vessels that Word flows through to arrive at the inner heart of the individual. Such illusions and deceit make of the Word a false power, deny the substantive nature of community, and prohibit women from speech. The Word, understood as the perfectly open sign dwelling with women on the margins of the social-symbolic order and of Christianity, cannot be disconnected from that which it continually creates, forms, funds, negates, transforms, and opens up. To deny the fullness of the relation of Word and community is to finalize a special gnosis in a secret club, which would prohibit Christians from speaking of emancipatory transformation in the world. The club of secret founding, apart from and beyond human community, is not the way of reordered relations, not service to the troubled world, not the restoration of creation, not transformation into glory. To deny the embodiment of Word in words, as the site where language, subjectivity, and politics are formed, is to deny the materialness of creation, the physicality of crucifixion and resurrection, the breath and fire of Spirit. The Word of God does not speak through empty vessels, but enlivens, creates, and forms the words of mind, heart, and soul in the openness of all hope.

By not receiving the Word in fullness and plenitude, as the perfectly open sign, the modern church limited, constrained, and distorted the poetics of community. In modernity, community has been reduced to aggregate collections, social clubs, life-style enclaves, and feel-good societies. In order to rend and renew the church through the rebirth of community, feminism must surround women-church with the Word received in the questions of women and in the visions of emancipatory transformation. The Word that forms community, that calls it into being and graces the horizons of its freedom, is the Word of plenitude, of embodiment, of creation. It is the Word which has long been the precondition of the Word of the order; it is the Word of multiplicity and difference, the Word of connection and desire. It is the Word which has been given to women, in the silences of their speaking: the Word which bridges nature and culture, laughter and weeping, solidarity and difference. This is the Word of the Bible, at least the Word which dances through the pages in dynamic relation, the Word that covers chaos and creation, the Word of relation in incarnation, crucifixion, and resurrection. The Bible discloses the dynamic character of this Word, that establishes connections and ruptures relations, that founds and destroys, that is death of all death and rebirth of all life.

The Word as perfectly open sign creates community by emancipatory transformation and as emancipatory transformation, enlivening, embodying, immersing, incarnating itself through the ways and means of communal life. The Word forms Christian community in its modeling of Christ as embodied Word, in its reading of the Scriptures as words of grace and hope, in its common spirit of Word as Spirit. Community, as woven together in the Word, is not unique, separate, or unconnected to all human relation, to flesh and blood, to need and desire. It is not conformed to the ways of the world which deny community, connections, bodies, and souls, but is transformed and restored in a community which is, at its heart, the ongoing communion of words and Word, of world and God, of life and Spirit.

The Word itself in its fullness, its connection, its creating, and its constant separation is in relation to community through communion, through the ongoing participation, remembering, anticipating, and feasting on the fullness of life itself. It is a communion that touches the body, the participation of nourishing sustenance, the recollection of solidarity with all, the anticipation of life fulfilled. The poetics of Word and community are not envisioned on the basis of the Word as the no which sets apart, divides, diminishes, dissuades, negates, but within the Word of plenitude, of participation, of nourishing, of acceptance, of all gathered around the table. Here, in communion with the Word, persons are nourished in the bread of life; persons are bonded together in the breaking of bread; persons are satisfied with the wine of new life; persons are laughing, sharing, and living—not in the negation of human life but in the fullness of life.[30] In this communion with the Word, women, long bakers of bread, nourishers of body, and preparers of the table, know and claim their access to the Word, the Word of plenitude, openness, hope, anticipation, suffering, struggle, silence, strength.

The Christian community is made in the Word and is bound together in the Word. The relation is not limited to a command or even an announcement. Rather, it is the "full sensorium of Word" to use the language of Walter Ong.[31] The poetics of communion displays the richness of words and Word in aesthetic envisioning, allowing the play of possibilities, memories, hopes, senses, and loves to blend together, to restore and to transform our lives. Ong suggests that when Abraham "heard" the voice of God, the auditory sense of hearing was selected because it seemed to describe Abraham's experience. So also does poetics suggest the Word of God, not through the word as visual, but with the mysterious, sacramental experience of sound: rich, manifest, dense, diverse, multiform, relational. As perfectly open sign, the Word surrounds us: connecting, relating, vibrating, resonating. The Word in this community in communion surrounds creation and chaos, wisdom and logos, life and death. The communion of emancipatory transformation in the community of the Word offers multiple possibilities of what humans can be—cast over creation and redemption—and it is thus a model of life lived with and for others.

Thus, as with Barth, a poetics of community begins by asking about the relation between community and Word. But in this beginning, in the space of women's marginality, a poetics of community as communion with Word forms to fund and continue feminism's poetics of community. No high steeples, no single word, no same announcement Sunday after Sunday. Rather the images explode in the aesthetic play of community, communion, Word, grace: women disciples speaking and being heard, memories of women recalled and celebrated, Deborah's song and Mary's Magnificat, Esther's beauty and Mary's adornment, chatting, laughing, weeping, singing, feasting. Images of participation, embodiment, mutuality, solidarity, Word mingling in words now and tomorrow rather than images of receptivity, passivity, pronouncement, foundations.

The poetics of community in communion with the Word is sacramental, the conveyor of grace. True community, nurtured and nourished by the Word which creates humans together, is the sacrament of the fullness of God's grace. It is the restoration of the basic elements of existence—the satisfaction of our senses, the exchange of words—into the transforming possibilities of life together where those gathered at the table are accepted in their differences, set free in their particularities, and graced into solidarity with the world. Grace comes not from an empty formality of existential acceptance, not in the rush of control in the marketplace, but in the blessing of community, for here the invisible presence of God is made visible, the fullness and abyss of God's love works through these relations in the freedom to speak—and in speaking freely—of emancipatory transformation for all.

The sacrament of communion, which the church at present observes as one ritual of cohesion, is, in the openness of the Word as perfectly open sign, the fullness of community itself. In the sacramentality of communion as community, the church is created as a community of poets, of poets who image, create, discover, and pursue the reordered relations of emancipatory transformation. Life, in Christian community, lives in communion with the Word expressing, creating, and forming new images, ways, forms, fashions. In this communion there is the imaging of life anew, the play of possibilities, the hope of dreams and vision. Community flourishes in its aesthetic practices, for every communicant is an artist creating and revisioning human flourishing in the specificity of her life. Art, poetry, song, dance, liturgy, theater, dreams, and visions are all the rebirthing of emancipatory transformation. Here is language itself set free to be in full communion, language which pushes at the boundaries of its limits, language which shatters the accepted ordering, which plays with new possibilities, which rends and renews through its own play.[32]

In the community of poets there is no mastery or control of poetics as a foundational enterprise. Feminism's poetics of the Word, the Word of community in communion, is characterized by what Fred Dallymar has called in reference to poetics and politics, gentleness and unconstraint.[33] The poetics of Word and community is characterized by the gentleness of being heard, and of speaking fully, of being full and of feeding others, of the fragility and possibility of life. The poetics of community is graced through the gentleness of the Word which does not place women away from community, but which embraces women into the midst of community. It is the unconstraint of love for the other that encourages and celebrates differences, the unconstraint that does not demand all persons be the same, the unconstraint that encourages all human flourishing. In the community of poets, the play of images moves across the experience in community as worship. It is the constant blurring of boundaries, the celebration of possibilities, the praise of God. Worship is the basis of community life only as this constant funding of images is explored and celebrated, for in this manner community is restored and transformed in the constant communion of words and Word.

This communion, this sacrament of grace, enables the community of poets to live in and through the proclamation of emancipatory transformation. For communion—the participation, the overflowing, of grace—revokes, rends, renews, and restores us into human life and transforms us anew in the horizon of all hope. The community of poets in gentleness and unconstraint will speak forth of community in many ways and spaces, including the imaging of universal community, community with the living and the dead, community with the future. This poetics must speak of community and communion within God, speaking of God in open, communicative relation.[34] Emancipatory transformation runs through the words and actions of the community of poets, leaping from the pages of the Scriptures, celebrating in songs and prayers, fermenting in missions and fellowships.

Life Together: The Rhetorical Nature of Community

Having restored community in communion with the Word and thus begun a formulation of the church in a poetics of communion, feminist theology must consider what this means for the nature of Christian community, or what can best be called the rhetorical nature of community. Feminist theology must turn, then, to what Schleiermacher called the corporate nature of the church and what Barth called the communion of saints, the gathering of the faithful, and the confederation of witnesses. What is the common life of the Christian community? What is this community in communion with the Word of plenitude, in solidarity with world, in communion with Word? What is this community as model of all community, as the intense manifestation of life together?

To speak of life together, in the midst of the poetics of this communion, is to consider again the Word and the Scriptures, but this time to consider them in the realm of human praxis, as lived, engaged, received, communicated, proclaimed in the midst of Christian community.[35] For Christianity lives with the Word and the Bible in community, the commonness, as Schleiermacher might say, formed in the Spirit. To consider community is to consider life together in ongoing relation to Word and Scriptures through emancipatory transformation.

To speak of community as life together in communion with the Word is to assert that through language and discourse the Word is embodied, revealed, expressed, and lived. In feminist theology Word and words are not opposed or separate, for by reconsidering women and the Word, feminism receives the Word in the fullness of grace. Within the reception of the fullness of this grace, feminism reconstructs community in the ongoing relations of Word and words, in embodiment, difference, specificity, anticipation, solidarity, and transformation. In the discussion of the community—in its constant deliberation through language that serves as the site of subjectivity, relationality, structures, and symbols—the Word is located and in turn locates the intersubjectivity of community. This incarnation of the Word exists through all the forms of communication in community: worship, education, fellowship, outreach, administration, care, counseling. In speaking freely together and in speaking through all that women are and do the Word becomes manifest. Community, born in this relation, created continually in its deliberation of life together, receives within itself the Bible.

The community in its life together deliberates continually in emancipatory transformation, weaving together its experiences, histories, hopes, problems, and dreams in relation to the Scriptures. While the Bible, at times, has had priority over community, and likewise Word, on occasion, has had priority against community and the Scriptures, in this text, through Word and vision, community lives in mutual relation with the Bible. The Bible does not form community, and community does not protect the Bible, but in ongoing relation the community and the Scriptures form life together.[36] The community lives together in deliberation through and in the Word with the Scriptures as resource, model, and vision. Community, in this text, receives from the Scriptures the proclamation of emancipatory transformation: the fullness of time and space in community, the reordered relations in the jubilee, the testimony of the prophet's life sealed to the discourse of freedom, and the freedom of Word in all words. The Scriptures are filled with prototypes of life together, demonstrating how communities receive the good news in and through the continual deliberation of life together.

This constant deliberation of life together in Word and with the Scriptures, is what we have alluded to as the rhetorical nature of community, the ongoing deliberation of who it is, what it does, where it is going, the nature of its past. For the community in communion with Word lives neither around a group of rules, nor as a collected group of individuals, nor, yet again, around a group of managerial practices. Instead, community in communion with Word lives in the intersubjectivity of community. What is needed for the community that proclaims is attention to the ongoing movement of its life; to the discourses of emancipatory transformation that constitute its practices and attitudes, its relations and discussions; and to its ways of naming both means and goals of the corporate nature. Rhetoric pays special attention to the relationship between the forms of action and the forms of discourses in the proclamation of emancipatory transformation.[37]

The modern church, as already considered, focused on the emotional needs of the individual, on the one hand, and the technical, instrumental reason of management practices on the other. Bereft of any attention to a substantive nature of community, the modern church could not consider how the proclamation of emancipatory transformation was shaped in its conversations and actions, its sermons and worship, its fellowship and practices *as a community*. For to attend to the community in communion with the Word, as a community, is to shift attention away from the individual and the bureaucratic toward the communal, and to focus on the community's deliberation of who it is, discerning what counts as common sense, revealing social practices and the relation of discourse to social practices, examining how fundamental attitudes are represented and expressed. What good reasons exist for this social-justice program? Why is this form of liturgy most appropriate for this group of people? What are the terms used to speak of human flourishing? The rhetorical nature of community locates the situationality of community (its embodiment in time and space), the intersubjectivity of community (its shared values, attitudes, and practices), and the transformation of community (its ongoing deliberation, change, and movement).

These questions of community, questions of dialogue, practice, deliberation, solidarity, and respect are, in the context of intersubjectivity, issues of rhetoric. Perhaps the trivialization of rhetoric in modernity is but the extension of the refusal to take community seriously. In the works of Aristotle, for instance, rhetoric is understood as the discourse of the *polis,* the reasoning and deliberation of the citizens to guide their common life. Rhetoric was the art of deliberation, the ongoing process of community life in communication of its ways, means, symbols, and acts.

In modernity, rhetoric is supposedly abandoned, coming to have only a negative meaning, as in "mere rhetoric," an opinion held without good reasons! Modernity counted as valid only those arguments that conformed to empirical facts. Descartes, regarded as the father of modern reason, noted in the first part of his logic that he intended to "take well nigh as false everything which was only plausible."[38] If modernity cast rhetoric aside, so also did community become distorted into collections of individuals and bureaucratic institutions. Without the ability to reason together, to deliberate its ongoing practices, any sense of substantive community languished. Likewise, without community, without the shared substance of ongoing conversation, shared visions, and common values, rhetoric could be but ornamental flourish.

In recent years, concern for rhetoric and community has again arisen. This has transpired at least in part through the critique of the historicalization of rationality. Ideology critique uncovered how rationality could take on a universal guise to cover particular interests of the few.[39] The shift in paradigms of knowledge, in both the hard and soft sciences, led to the recognition of the social basis of rationality.[40] Various movements in deconstruction and poststructuralism have analyzed the relation of reason and power. Indeed, in the present situation, there may well be consensus with Terry Eagleton's verdict, "Rhetoric, in other words, precedes logic: grasping propositions is only possible in specific forms of social life."[41]

Yet another way to cast an analysis of modernity is to consider the deceitful figuration of its major metaphors and tropes: mastery, success, presence, autonomy, and progress. Ways of speaking have been structured into the ways of acting, and vice versa; ways of being in the world have developed out of and in constant close relation to ways of speaking.[42] For figures of speech so beloved in modernity prevent and prohibit solidarity, differences, life together, future life, anticipatory freedom, and open hope. Yet a simple assertion of need for rhetoric will be no more helpful than the gleeful pointing out that, despite modernity's language, its logic too was grounded in large part in rhetorical figures, assumptions, and certain historical practices that were neither empirically or metaphysically necessary.

To transform the practices and discourses of modernity—practices and discourses that prohibit community and, thus, solidarity, difference, dialogue, and deliberation—it is necessary to avoid moving backward to a place where rhetoric is tied to free citizens as men of property, but to move forward to a place where community is inclusive of all persons. Feminism moves the church forward by discovering and creating the possibilities of community, wherein women and men may engage in the rhetorical practice of life together in just and fair deliberation. Within the desire of modernity for community, in our relation to the Word as perfectly open sign and the Scriptures as prototypes of proclamation, feminist theology must find, from the positionality of women, a rhetorical nature of community that is conducive to emancipatory transformation. The rhetorical nature of Christian community cannot be just any deliberation but must always be the ongoing deliberation of emancipatory transformation.[43] The rhetorical nature of Christian community constitutes itself through and in its own proclamation.

A great deal is already known about the proclamation of emancipatory transformation and what this means for Christian community. Such proclamation is graced in its differences and its solidarity, blessed in its anticipation and transformation. In such proclamation, the community reads the Scriptures, hears the tradition, and, most importantly, lives in relation to the Word. This community does not just happen in space and time, an empty vessel for the meeting place of God and human, but is constituted in the space and time of Word and words. In this view of community and book, hermeneutics (the interpretation of the Scriptures) takes place in the context of rhetoric, the deliberation of life together, and rhetoric names the relation of Word, Bible, and community in the praxis of life together.[44] The proclamation of emancipatory transformation names the rhetorical nature of Christian community, the corporate nature of Christian life: in deliberation, conversation, and dialogue that grows out of connections and differences, out of intersubjectivity, out of ongoing participation in emancipatory transformation.

The proclamation of emancipatory transformation as the rhetorical nature of Christian community emphasizes both differences and solidarity, for solidarity is possible only when differences are accepted and affirmed. There is no one way of being human, no one way of faith: multiplicity, particularity, and specificity are all qualities of Christian community. Community is enriched by differences, for only with the richness of this texture of community can there be visions of human flourishing. Indeed, this community does not merely tolerate differences, it demands, enables, and encourages differences. This community promotes differences within each person as well as differences between persons; rules of identity as autonomous agents of suffocation are put aside with the blessing and grace of Word as communion. Amid these differences solidarity arises, a solidarity that takes time, patience, care, and gentleness—one that knows conflict, one that enlivens opposition, but one that also nurtures solidarity through differences and conflicts. This is a community of solidarity, a community of being with and being for, a community whose solidarity is so much the warp of its texture, that the intensity of presence is nurtured and nourished.

This is also a community of anticipation and transformation. Not simply a community that anticipates and transforms, that moves out into the world to change and correct, to predict and promote, but a community whose texture is one of anticipation and transformation, a community that deliberates and decides. What is it to anticipate but to wonder, to query, to question, to probe, to deliberate, to decide? This is a community that deliberates what could be, what may be. It is a community that thus overflows with visions: visions of peace, visions of justice, visions of harmony with the earth, visions of cultural regeneration. And in these visions and with these visions, it continually transforms and is transformed. For this community is not static and staid, it does not exist merely as a building where individuals may be gathered or bureaucracy may be housed. First and foremost this community acts in its life together: worship, service, care, mission, ethics. And all these practices are corporate ways and means of transformation, the ongoing practice of life together in community.

In the marginality of women-church, then, with Word as a perfectly open sign, there is a place to reconstruct, in relation to Schleiermacher and Barth, life together in Christian community. By reconstructing life together as rhetorical, feminist theology emphasizes the situatedness, fluidity, and creativity of all discourse and the importance of being in dialogue with the Scriptures and in communion with the Word. By exploring community as the intersubjectivity of life in words and Word, in history and Spirit, feminist theology suggests that this intersubjectivity is characterized by a fundamental openness and solidarity in differences that lives through constant deliberation. The proclamation of emancipatory transformation, as life within Christian community, involves the ongoing deliberation of life together, the celebration of communion with Word, the interpretation of the Scriptures, the acts of service, protest, formation, and leisure. Enlivened by Word and the Scriptures, Christian community deliberates the practical possibilities of emancipatory transformation, for only in particular historical practices can emancipatory transformation, if it is to be also proclaimed to the world, constitute the forms of life in community.

The rhetorical nature of community explores the texture of its solidarity by affirming differences and specificities as well as connections and relations. In a dialogical community, rhetoric forms and informs character and virtue, interpretations and performances, acts and services, across the many levels of communal life. But here, in ongoing discourse and dialogue, the freedom to speak is nourished and strengthened; here in the back and forth, around and about, detour and rambling, speaking freely is encouraged and demanded. In this fashion emancipatory transformation occurs in the rhetorical practices of community, in communion with the Word and in freedom with and for each other.

The Spirit of Community

Proclamation is the discourse of the community, the ongoing communication of emancipatory transformation in the life together of the believers. Bible, community, and Word all exist together in the rhetorical life of community—its configuration of life, its deliberation of practices, its celebration of hope. Throughout modernity proclamation has been narrowly understood as the church proclaiming the Word to unbelievers only for the moment of conversion, or proclaiming the Word to believers only for existential or moral sustenance. Yet time and time again, this has narrowed the Word and emptied proclamation, making the communication of God and Word, the communion of community without the richness of the embodied, openness, the fullness of Word and the vision, the hope, the questioning of the Scriptures. Thus feminist theology forms proclamation as the discourse of freedom that Christian community gives to the world through the Word, through the visions of the Scriptures, and through the ongoing poetics and rhetoric of community itself. Now it is possible to approach the final step in the theological reconstruction of Christian community in speaking of the piety of the community, finishing in the fashion of Schleiermacher, by suggesting that piety arises in the corporate nature of community.

Out of community, formed in the plenitude of the communion with the Word and fashioned in the communication of life together, arises the living of the Christian life, the structures of Christian existence. In this text, which but claims the commonness of Spirit, community, and believers in a preliminary way, fashioned of the marginality of the "other" and the unmet desires in and on the margins of the social-symbolic order, it is almost impossible to suggest what this life of grace might look like. Feminism has hints, promises, musings, and hopes for a life of grace that includes the grace to live differently, the grace to question and to resist, the grace to anticipate and transform, the grace to celebrate and to mourn.[45] The piety arising in the Spirit with the common spirit of community, amid the themes and resonances of Word and Scriptures, will affirm difference and connections, the fullness of time, the movement of solidarity, particularity and commonness.

Such piety emerges only in the union of Spirit with the spirit of community. At this point, in light of the difficulty of forming images of community and forms of community that allow the plenitude of communion and life together in community, it is possible only to signify four gifts of the Spirit that must arise out of community in order for community itself to exist: justice, vitality, wisdom, and love. These gifts, in the union of the Spirit and the spirit of life together, serve as criteria, involving the practices of speaking, and also as virtues, that which community nourishes in dialogue. Seen as intrinsic to conversation itself, they are the goals of Christian life together.

Justice is the gift of the Holy Spirit that means, first of all, that all have equal access to speak, and equal rights to deliberate and converse in community.[46] It is not enough, for instance, to give women access to the debate in community and then demand that they use the same terms and arguments that have been used to oppress them. Justice is openness to all and accessibility of all to deliberation. The just person is the person who stands with others, in solidarity, the person who hears others into speech, the person who continually forms new possibilities of emancipatory transformation in community.

Vitality, or creativity, is the gift of freshness, newness, artistic vision. Vitality is rendering anew the reading of the Scriptures, forming anew the prayers of the community, creating new possibilities of celebration.[47] Necessary for community lest it not accept the ongoing power of resurrection in the Spirit which creates life anew, vitality may question even the forms of the criterion of justice, rupturing, opposing, or circumventing that which has been considered as appropriate or adequate. The vital person is one who sings new songs, who knows the riskiness of faith, who holds the experiment as open and good, who embraces differences in the richness of the plenitude of the Spirit.

Wisdom is the gift of knowing what is fitting, of what is credible and appropriate.[48] Wisdom knows the tales of the past, but also sees visions of the future. Wisdom, knowing both general principles and the specificity of the particular, is *prudentia,* the prudence of judging the fittingness of factors involved. The wise person, in the community's life together, will be revered as one who can guide the community to the best use of resources, to the best form of celebration, to the most insightful decision.

The final gift of the Spirit in Christian piety is love. Of all the gifts, love may be the hardest of all to name, but undeniably, even as Paul thought, the most important. Love is listening with a sensitive ear to others' pain, love is moving with others in glorification of God. Love is a solidarity which forsakes one's own riches to take on another's burdens; love is, as Bonhoeffer said of grace, costly.[49] In terms of the rhetorical life of community, love is the willingness to engage in open, free conversation; the willingness to accept and celebrate difference; the willingness to let one's mind be changed; the willingness to make one's own opinion, argument, and knowledge available. The person who has the virtue of love, in the power of the Spirit, is one who partakes, risks, and gives fully; the one who is persuasive and open to persuasion, the one whose gift of love opens her or him fully to the ongoing conversation in the community.

This gift of love is the greatest of all if, today, feminists are to rend and renew the church as a community of emancipatory transformation. The very way of defining, constructing, and approaching the church must be discovered anew in a formulation of community that brings together the poetics of communion, the rhetoric of life together, and the gifts of the Spirit. Thus the diversity, situationality, and complexity of each community must be respected; but also the commonness and the shared vision in developing ways to speak of freedom by freely speaking must be recognized as Christian communities, formed in the visions of women-church, seek to proclaim good news to the world.

· 4 ·

PROCLAMATION AS THE WORD FOR THE WORLD

To be in the margin is to be part of the whole but outside the main body.

Bell Hooks

He said: foot, boot, order, city, fist, roads, time, knife.

She said: water, night, willow, rope hair, earth belly, cave, meat, shroud, open, blood.
They both kept their promises.

Margaret Atwood

My words now must be as slow, as new, as single, as tentative as the steps I took going down the path away from the house, between the dark-branching tall dancers motionless against the winter shining.

Ursula K. Le Guin

In the discourses of feminist theology, proclamation is not formed around an eternally finished content nor understood through an a priori theory that works for all times and places. It is, rather, radically immanent in the world existing in the margins and gaps of present structures, in the dances and laughter of women as well as in the visions and hopes of the poor, in the desires for love and relatedness of the bourgeoisie, in the poetry and dreams of people of color. Proclamation comprises new visions of the main body, visions of earth, night, cave; images that give, gingerly and tentatively, words of freedom to freely speak. To recognize this means also to recognize that proclamation is always partial, for such is the nature of the historicity of language that any view of the world can be only relatively adequate, for all words of freedom must come from the particularity and specificity of where women stand to speak. This is the command and gift of discipleship, to stand and speak in this time and place, not with complete knowledge or within a totalized theory, but between the faith of God's community and the grace of being in solidarity with the world in the Word.

In this final chapter examining the proclamation of Word *to* and *for* the world, it is necessary to proceed, first, by suggesting one analysis of the present social-symbolic ordering. Christianity has often gained its power by the analysis of sin, the interpretation of how, in the receptivity of its visions and stories, it understands the world in that time and place. There is, in the procedures of this text, no one ahistorical view of humanity's fallenness. Instead, a contextual reading will be offered, since to proclaim emancipatory transformation depends, at least in part, on the disclosing power of an analysis of destruction, distortion, and death. In this text, a critical reading will focus on a "grand theory," an interpretive analytics of the ordering of language, subjectivity, and politics. This is but one reading, one in relation to the rhythms of emancipatory transformation which, through feminism's semiotics and pragmatics deals with visions of transformation.

Between critical analysis and proclamation to the world, a place must exist from which to rend and renew the social-symbolic order. This text has argued for such a place in the relations between feminism and Christianity because the voices and power of women are a reality of resistance and transformation, a reality that can both rend and renew the present situation. Such an argument presupposes a particular view of feminism and feminist theology, one in which women use their marginality to pursue possibilities of transformation through discourses of emancipatory transformation. Though this view of feminism and feminist theology affirms and accents multiple voices and strategies, it does so by arguing that feminist theology must not remain mortgaged to the dominant social-symbolic order. The second step of this chapter is to articulate this view of feminism and feminist theology, and to define it in relation to other forms of feminism.

After articulating feminist theology in the space of resistance and transformation, this chapter explores both present and possible resources in the marginality of women for proclaiming the Word to and for the world. Resources, rather than polished discourses, must be imposed as the internal limit in this text, for the contours of feminist proclamations must arise in conversations together, beyond the possibilities set by this provisional text. But given the reading of the social-symbolic ordering, and the revisioning of feminism, it is possible to identify sources of emancipatory transformation that arise in feminism so conceived, and what such sources suggest for creating and discovering new ways of speaking of freedom and new ways of speaking freely. These are, as were the movements in the poetics and rhetorics of ecclesiology, imagistic in character, for when women are questioning the fundamental forms of the social-symbolic order, they must begin through images that both push at the limits and proffer new ways of human flourishing. Feminist theology, as conceived in this book, pursues a transformation that language works hard at concealing, and the categories of emancipatory transformation can be arrived at only through a resistance which is, at the same time, also an imagistic renewal.

Finally, after identifying resources to proclaim Word to and for the world, this chapter considers more explicitly the relation of the resources in feminism to the grand theory of language, subjectivity, and politics, though these possible relations, of course, have been implicit all along. While the exploratory nature of this text—of speaking in the margins and gaps through the Word as perfectly open sign, in a community that is as much a dream as a reality, in the Scriptures received through a hermeneutics of marginality—encourages dreams of and desires for such proclamations, it also suggests some ways to cast feminism's critique and vision, for the proclamation of Word to and for the world seeks to transform the social-symbolic order by providing not only new images of human flourishing, but new ways of imaging and speaking.

Language, Subjectivity, and Politics

How are we to characterize, to describe, no matter how partially, the world in which we live? Death, control, destruction, deviance, force, manipulation, murder. These terms, these words, label the end of the modern era, the era of freedom, progress, and reason. If there are history books in the future, of what will they speak, what events will they find symbolic—the progress of science that leads to Hiroshima or the not-yet nuclear apocalypse that looms to explode us all as dust unto dust, having finally managed unto ashes the fragile force of life?[1] In what manner will future history books speak of the modern state, guarantor of the Enlightenment, with its hatred of the Jew suppressed through reason and representation, finally made manifest in the Holocaust?[2] Such events rupture discourse even in the present situation, they are fundamentally unrepresentable in the magnitude of their horror. The mimetic or even descriptive language used to report such events suggests already an enlightened history in which torture and repression are more common than aid and refuge.[3] The demonic power of destruction and force, threatening nature, society, and subjectivity, is co-present with the mania of psychic oppressiveness: failure, suicide, stress, psychosis, drug addiction, depression, and schizophrenia stalk the present age.[4]

It is imperative not to equate, of course, events of violence with the violent breakdown of psychic identity. Death camps, atomic bombs, and apartheid are not here equated with the distraught psyche of the bourgeois individual. To have to protest against such an objection already indicates a massive rule of identity where events, individuals, and history have an origin, a norm, and a principle in which all events, ideas, persons, and moments can fit. Rather, I use the term co-present with full seriousness to describe the world in which I live and to which I must speak. This world is described by both political theologians and liberation theologians who seek to give voice to human suffering. Political theologians attempt to expose the violence of the psychic destruction of the middle-class subject.[5] Yet such psychic destruction is not to be seen as separate from the radical destruction of the "others" of history, presented in the work of liberation theologians, who seek to be the voice of the poor and oppressed.[6] These voices of the subjects who suffer history and the subjects who control history are interwoven, forming the warp of our lives, the weft of our history.

By bringing together, not through any principle of causal efficacy but through a delicate and fragile coupling, events of suffering with the destruction of psychic identity, it is possible to begin to uncover, hesitantly and haltingly, the interwoven pattern of the dominant social-symbolic order.[7] Indeed, as discourses of emancipatory transformation, proclamation must include analysis of the social-symbolic order in its implications for both psychic structures and historical events; only in this unmasking may judgment be expressed as grace. Proclamation must say no to the practices of history in the midst of God's yes to the possibilities of the world. What judgment and transformation consist of, in this day and age, in these embattled and forlorn times, is to show the relation of language, politics, and subjectivity in the dominant social-symbolic order and, standing on the margins and in the breaks of that order, to glimpse and whisper possibilities of transformation. Furthermore, as discourses of freedom, proclamation must protest against oppressiveness and repressiveness through practices of insurrection, be they boycotts, prayers, fasts, alternative life-styles, legislative changes, or other forms of subversion. Issues such as nuclear destruction, depression, third world–first world relations, and aging all provide places to stand from which to capture a view of the social-symbolic order, places to render judgment in the midst of grace.

In order to stand and speak, some attempt to grasp a broad portrayal of the present situation seems necessary. One such way is to use, in a tentative and hypothetical fashion, the tools of what can be called a "grand theory," a broad-based interpretive analysis that moves across the discursive and nondiscursive practices of the present. It is necessary not to remain in any one "grand theory" too long for they are helpful only insofar as they allow the distance necessary to make critiques broad enough and deep enough. Without a theoretical hypothesis or framework, critiques on any particular topic tend too easily to be surface sketches. Thus, without explaining the psychic constitution of narcissistic subjectivity, a critique of world poverty turns victims into numbers, represented by an instrumentalist language and whims of political structure, all seen as beyond human control. Likewise, not to view the psychological violence today in major disorders such as depression without understanding the political ordering forces the analysand to become adapted to a situation which itself is dangerously distorted. My plea is difficult but nonetheless important: though proclamation must be particular, it must also be done in relation to a broad and deep analysis of the ordering of systems and consciousness that uncovers the relations, the anonymous rules, the hidden principles in language, subjectivity, and politics. With one such analysis, suggested here as only one partial view, it is important to begin before turning to the margins of the social-symbolic order and the particular margins held by women, to offer one possibility of proclamation for the world.

Language, subjectivity, and politics: these three realms, dimensions, common places, form today the structuring of the dominant social-symbolic order and provide the problems and possibilities of transformation. They do not, of course, fit neatly together, nor can they be strictly defined. Though language has been given priority in this text, understood as the site of both subjectivity and politics, it is important to underscore that neither subjectivity nor politics is reducible to language. Though language is the tool of this book's attempt to rend and renew the social-symbolic order, it is necessary to form the analysis of the social-symbolic order through politics and subjectivity as well.[8] In this manner broad sketches can be drawn that name the economies that dominate the basic themes and rules in modernity: in language, representational discourse; in subjectivity, narcissistic patterning; in politics, self-preservation.

Language, as understood in this book, is essential to social relations and subjectivity. Indeed, Christian theology has recognized this, in some form or another, in other periods and situations. Augustine demonstrated, in the first chapter of his *Confessions,* that language is both the entrance into subjectivity and the entrance into social relations. For Augustine, the acquisition of language, wherein the body is broken by punishment and the soul desires to flee, marks the difference between the baby whose needs are anticipated by the mother or nurse and the child who is subject to the social-symbolic order:

> So by hearing words arranged in various phrases and constantly repeated, I gradually pieced together what they stood for, and when my tongue had mastered the pronounciation, I began to express my wishes by means of them. In this way I made my wants known to my family and they made their wants known to me and I took a further step into the stormy life of human society, although I was still subject to the authority of my parents and the will of my elders.[9]

But language itself, in its own historical formulations, has different functions, shapes, and dimensions; language means differently in different times.[10] On the one hand, this is mere common sense; it is obvious that the exclamation "O my God" can be used to express praise, joy, exasperation, terror, or surprise. On the other hand, this claim suggests that language has been formed and used differently in different historical periods and if the claim about the interrelations of language, subjectivity, and politics is correct, then subjectivity and politics, just as language, can be formed differently at different times. Language, in the social-symbolic order of modernity, can be termed "representational discourse," meaning that language re-presents, or presents again, the consciousness of the subject.[11] Language functions to express the "real" meaning of a thing, the meaning given to it in the consciousness of the subject. By comparison, in the Middle Ages language revealed, through its unity with the created order, the many facets of a sacramental world. Thus bread and wine could become flesh because, linguistically speaking, all participated in the substance of a manifest and created order. But, in the dominant ordering of modernity, bread and wine can only mean by re-calling to consciousness the already determined understanding of the eucharistic event. In the modern view, language is neither a mirror of God nor of nature but of the autonomous ego.

It is, likewise, this turn to a particular construct of the individual, a construct in which the identity of the individual is knowable and representable, that constitutes the subjectivity of the modern order, a subjectivity that no one ultimately can have, but that all desire and are judged by. So defined is subjectivity by the individual self that the very term *subject*, on occasion, is understood to be the problem.[12] Modern subjectivity, the very nature of experiencing the world through the lens of the autonomous ego, is labeled by many analysts and critics as narcissistic.[13]

Narcissus, it may be recalled, was a beautiful youth of Greek mythology, who, filled with pride, refused to let others near him. Echo, one of the many nymphs who loved Narcissus, wasted away in Narcissus's scorn. Dying, Echo was heard by another scorned lover, and this lover prayed to Neimesis that Narcissus would one day fall in love with someone who would not return that love; the desire was granted. One day Narcissus bent to drink from a pool and his gaze fell upon the most beautiful youth he had ever seen. Narcissus fell in love with the image reflected in the pool with no awareness that he was, in fact, enamored with his own reflection. Unable to reach the one he had finally found worthy of his desire, indeed in love with an image that could not return his affection, Narcissus grew distraught and sought to leave his physical body. Indeed, at Narcissus's funeral, no body could be found; a flower, named forever after the one who could love only his own image, was found in his place.

Modern narcissism longs and pines away for its own reflection, seeking a freedom separate from the body, a reason and a morality universally above all history. Modern subjectivity, living fully and responsibly, must turn inward to guide the sensible world; in this, experience is conformed to self-consciousness, the world to the inner workings of space and time. The self desires the illusion of the self, the concupiscent fantasy of knowing and controlling the world. In theology, anthropology becomes now the referent to interpret Christian symbols and doctrines. For instance, in some forms of liberal protestant Christianity, Calvin's version of the knowledge of the self in light of the knowledge of God becomes an idea of the referential imagination: since without knowledge of the self there is no knowledge, God must be spoken of as a referent of the knowledge the self has of itself. Alternatively stated, in modernity God is a condition of human imagination, a moral law within the individual; Christianity becomes the highest form of religion and religion a sublime form of humanism.

This subject that knows and lives unto itself contracts to live in society, and its politics become a vicious cycle of self-preservation both in terms of protecting autonomous selves and in terms of protecting the state as an autonomous reality.[14] Modern politics depends upon the understanding that the autonomous individual freely chooses to enter into relationships with other autonomous individuals. Each individual who voluntarily chooses to associate with others is a proprietor of his own person and abilities.[15] As such, society is gathered around market relations, or as C. B. Macpherson has noted, "Political society is a human contrivance for the protection of the individual's property in his person and good, and (therefore) for the maintenance of orderly relations of exchange between individuals regarded as proprietors of themselves."[16] Politics depends on three basic conditions: (1) the distinction between the public and private realms, (2) the divisions between economic classes, and (3) competitive relations in which each individual pursues his own interests. The fundamental goal of the political is to preserve the rights of the individual, and this goal is linked to an isolated subjectivity and a representational language, forming preservation as itself the goal of the state. As the state functions to preserve the rights of the individual, so it takes on a life of its own as an autonomous entity, cooperating and competing with other states for its own self-preservation.

It is, of course, "more complicated than that," and these complicating factors provide, at least in part, the possibilities of transformation.[17] But such an interpretive analysis provides a way of asking questions, a set of terms in which to understand and hopefully to understand differently. To question the duplicity of representational language, of narcissistic subjectivity, and of the self-preservation of the political, is not to suggest that there are not other understandings and realities of language, subjectivity, and politics. But it is to suggest that these understandings, in a relatively adequate fashion, constitute and represent the dominant ordering and are, today, subject to resistance and transformation in the discourses of freedom from the margins and fissures of the social-symbolic order.

Language, subjectivity, and politics cannot simply be done away with. Indeed, the only possible route for survival is resistance to and transformation of the rules, principles, orderings, and substance of language, subjectivity, and politics. But such resistance and transformation can occur only by finding places where subjectivity, language, and politics have existed in somewhat different fashion as "other" and by pursuing the transformation of these possibilities for the emancipatory transformation of all. The positionality of women provides one such space to explore subjectivity, politics, and language, but such an exploration itself depends upon carefully examining the status of critique and vision from this space of possibility.

Feminism and Patriarchal-Monotheistic Ordering

Until recently, feminist analysis in Christianity, as in feminism in general, has moved between two spaces: one I will call liberal egalitarianism and the other I will call romantic expressivism; both determined, in a sense, by the dictates of the social-symbolic order.[18] In the first space, feminists have used the aims and categories of modern liberal theory to argue women's right of equal access to the social-symbolic order and thus to ensure their full humanity. In the second space, feminists have used the "unique" subjectivity of woman as defined by the social-symbolic order to speak of woman's particularity in a suggested separation from the masculine constitution of the subject. Neither has fully examined the depth of the social-symbolic order in its explicitly Christian form or in its "secularized" version of modernity. Today, a third option is emerging that focuses on women's marginality to the social-symbolic order in order to offer discourses of emancipatory transformation. These discourses allow the marginal space of women to be a place of critique and transformation of the social-symbolic order, in regard not simply to the status and role of women but also to hidden principles and practices that figure and enforce otherness and multiplicity as taboo and chaos. Such discourses depend, however, on dissolving the loyalty of feminism to the patriarchal-monotheistic ordering of modernity, in order to identify further resources for emancipatory transformation that today proclaim the Word to and for the world.[19]

In the space of liberal egalitarianism, the greatest political gains have been made using liberal claims and terms to argue for the rights of women in public arenas, and, in the academy, to argue for political ends of scholarship. But the result of these considerable gains has been an awkward contradiction for some women, perhaps an erasure of the question for most women, in relation to any real gains in determining new roles for women in modernity. Liberal egalitarianism, that which has occupied the main role of feminism in politics and in religion, uses the terms and limits of liberalism to advocate the inclusion of women, but fails to question the patriarchal basis of liberalism, a basis that denies the inclusion of women.[20] Liberalism is the political ordering in modernity of individual autonomy and, in the market relations of society, the preservation of equal opportunity for individuals. Having been constructed on the patriarchal ordering of the public and private realms, liberalism results in the mystification of the dependence of the autonomous individual in the public realm upon the family unit in the private realm.[21] The point is that the political ordering of women and the family in the private realm exists as a historical necessity for the practices of liberalism.

A contradiction in the feminist use of liberal theories of equality and freedom arises from a failure to understand the liberal mystification of the political ordering of women and the family. Feminists have used liberal claims about equal rights to place women in professions, to work for affirmative action, and to assert the equality of women with men. Yet though there has been some success, at least in principle, in getting women into professions and public roles of society, there has been relatively little change in the patriarchal ordering of the private and the public. The success of liberal egalitarianism has been limited to minimal opportunities for a few women to enter professions; women who do enter traditionally male professions find themselves operating, time and time again, like men. Most women who choose to work outside the home must take low-paying jobs of institutional mothering such as nursing, teaching, and secretarial work that merely continue in the public realm what women do in the private realm.

The contradiction implicit in liberal egalitarianism is that the few women who can enter men's professions are forced to act like men to be fully human in the public realm. However, opening up the possibilities for women to move out of the private realm does not change the patriarchal ordering for the majority of women. Liberal egalitarianism fails to recognize that liberalism is itself embedded in a patriarchal ordering between the public and the private, an ordering that grounds liberalism upon the defining of separate, unequal spaces for men and women in which men represent the public space, the place of referentiality, control, and decision, that which is promoted in monotheistic ordering, while women are contained in the margins of the private realm, the place of relatedness, difference, embodiment, that which is taboo and set apart in monotheistic ordering.

Feminist scholarship represents a particular instance in liberal egalitarianism of the failure to question deeply enough the ordering of humanistic scholarship. Working within the humanistic belief in the identity of "man" who expresses his unique individuality in art, history, and politics, feminist theorists have been able to show that the methods of humanism speak not for a universal subject but for one who is universalized as the preserved subject of the dominant order. As Toril Moi has argued, the paradox in the strategy of unmasking the power relations in humanism is that feminist scholarship remains mortgaged to humanist methods and is thus unable to be radical enough: "its radical analysis of sexual politics still remains entangled with depoliticizing theoretical paradigms."[22] The problem gets even more complicated when feminists attempt to employ the methods of humanism for their scholarship. At most, and even this rarely happens, feminist scholars, by using the accepted categories of the social-symbolic order, argue for the inclusion of women's experience, experience both denied and ordered by the social-symbolic order, as correctives of that order. Like the liberal feminist working in affirmative action, the feminist scholar working with humanism's methods gets caught in the deceitful relation between patriarchal oppression and liberal preservation. Furthermore, for the few women (academics or other professionals) who use the categories of humanism for their own political ends, the question inevitably arises: What *do* women bring that is unique; once invited and allowed in, do women proffer anything different from what men offer?

The feminism of romantic expressivism seems to supply a possible answer, though I must hasten to add that this response exists for women who stay within the confines of the liberal ethos, including mainline Christianity. Other women, frustrated by the rigidity of the political order, turn to romantic expressivism as a form of separateness; a certain romanticization of the difference between women and men, and hence attention to the unique and untainted qualities of women is, for some, the starting position.[23] Such a position is not logically or historically an outgrowth of the failure of liberal egalitarianism; it is more directly related to a romantic embracement of the psychic relief offered as a separate location from the social-symbolic order. Yet, in Christian feminist discourse, a version of this position is often grafted onto liberal egalitarianism as a way to cover the contradiction revealed in liberal egalitarianism. Romantic expressivism claims that women have unique gifts, talents, personalities, and inhabitations of the world. Women, so the romantic expressivist contends, are uniquely women, and this uniqueness is often based on allusions to biological or metaphysical principles. Women, according to the feminism of romantic expressivism, excell in nurturing, warmth, noncompetition, relationality, peace, nature, and patience. All these characteristics are assigned to women by the present form of patriarchy and are celebrated by romantic expressivism as women's unique gifts. When liberal egalitarianism seeks to figure out what difference it does or should make to have women in the public arena, it often moves to a position of romantic expressivism. When trying to suggest a corrective that women might bring to the order, the liberal egalitarian will suggest, for instance, that women will not be as authoritarian as men in preaching and church administration. Or, as noted above, some women simply locate themselves in the position of romantic expressivism, leaving Christianity altogether and living in a separate women's space, assuming that one simply can choose to leave the linguistic, subjective, and political structures of the social-symbolic order. This is, of course, quite the problem with the feminism of romantic expressivism: the assumption that one can take the underbelly of the social-symbolic order and make it dominant or separable.[24] This position assumes that women's experience can be dislocated from the order, that women's experience has its own essence which can be put forth as a new order. Yet, women who try to function or live in this womanly way discover, too often, that it is impossible to do so, finding themselves caught in the interlacing structures of the need for patriarchal support.

One place to begin an analysis of how feminism has failed, until recently, to question the ordering, and not merely the effects, of modernity is by looking at what appears, at least in one's first acquaintance with feminism, to be the most radical contention of feminist theology: the challenge to the metaphor of God the Father and the shift to include new metaphors, including the metaphor of God as Mother. Changing the most basic of all metaphors should have a linchpin effect, since if one alters the key term of a system, other changes should result necessarily. But because feminist theology has failed, at least in large part, to question how metaphors work, and, correlatively, how any term for God works in the ordering of modernity, the radical contribution is muffled, becoming yet another strategy of inclusive correction in modern Christian discourse.

The analysis is centered around a question: Does God as the Father fundamentally function as a metaphor in representational language?[25] What is required to answer yes to this question is first an understanding of language where metaphors can be adapted by an act of will, an understanding that views language itself as metaphorical in a particular fashion. This view is dependent upon understanding language as representational, where language represents what the speaker intends or means. Metaphor is doubly useful in representational language, both because it allows multiple meanings, and because its meaning is always determined as a referent of the individual. Thus God is like a father and God is like a mother, but God is still, of course, the referent, the representation of what it is to be fully or authentically human. This understanding of metaphor protects the representational character of our discourse and, naturally in this view, if one intends to image God as mother, one simply needs to shift the metaphors.[26]

Yet this seems, at least to many, highly unsatisfactory. Some can, of course, pray to God the Mother and at least most potentially can recognize maternal, or feminine, images of God in the Bible. But the question must be raised as to why it is so difficult to say, "O God our Mother," and why it is so startling to uncover scriptural images suggestive of God as a woman.[27] To begin, in this way, is to move to the issue of the social-symbolic ordering, to suggest that language has, not only images, but a certain economy, that it itself is ordered symbolically, and that God the Father is more than a metaphor that can be changed at will. No matter what the images or metaphors are or can be, there is a deep symbolic economy in culture that separates, as it divides, the name of the Father and the order it represents with what is configured as "woman" and the chaos she represents. In this symbolic economy, which regulates and forms subjectivity, the ordering of language is again and again characterized by the name of the Father. Father is thus not only a metaphor but a law and an ordering: Father regulates the law of separation and division, obedience and submission to the governing order. In one sense "Father" is a metaphor but it is a metaphor for God, and God is determined in a fatherly way as the determination of the patriarchal order, *fatherly* here being defined as that which orders, determines, divides, and demands loyalty to a way of representation, preservation, and identity. Feminists can add all the metaphors they want, provided they represent this fatherly configuration of God in language, securing patriarchy, and the fatherly ordering of language, preserving monotheism.

This ordering, that has been explored already in the semiotics of the Word, is a monotheistic ordering, that forces language, as well as politics and subjectivity, to operate according to sexual, hierarchical rules.[28] What has already been discovered to be true about the monotheistic ordering of the Word in theological discourse operates insidiously through the ordering of language, politics, and subjectivity—operates, indeed, through the social-symbolic order itself. What feminism has often failed to realize is that patriarchy is not merely an implication of how politics is applied, how language is used, how subjectivity is expressed, but how language, politics, and subjectivity are constituted in patriarchy through monotheistic ordering. But the realization that patriarchy is constituted and extended through the forming of subjectivity, politics, and language (though not entirely determining them) allows feminism not only an understanding of women's complicity in their oppression, but also an appreciation of women's pleasure as well as pain in patriarchy and, in addition, an identification of new sources for resistance and transformation.

The monotheistic ordering of patriarchy means that God the Father is the agent of rule through separation and division, a rule which secures, through patrilineal descent, the place of women's role: the procreation of the species. The only possibility, given the present symbolic economy, for the Mother to be equated in image with the Father, and thus adopted as a new metaphor for God, the highest term of entitlement, would be if the Mother could become a maternalized version of the Father. But in the deep symbolic economy of monotheism, now secularized in the modern state, God the Father functions as a ruling sovereign that is, quite literally, the continuing division and separation of the social-symbolic order that secures the identity of the subject, the representation of language, the self-preservation of the political.

I am suggesting, in other words, that feminist theology must examine the monotheistic ordering of the social-symbolic economy. This monotheistic ordering, running through secularized forms of language, subjectivity, and politics resounds with a deeply religious economy dominant in Christianity. In order to proclaim God to and for the world, feminist theology must pursue the unmasking of, resistance to, and transformation of this monotheistic ordering, for as Julia Kristeva has observed:

> At best one is guilty of naïvety if one considers our modern societies as simply patrilineal, or class-structured, or capitalist-monopolist, and omits the fact that they are at the same time (and never one without the other) governed by a monotheism whose essence is best expressed in the Bible: the 'paternal Word' sustained by a fight to the death between the two races (men/women). In this naïvety, one forgets that whatever attacks this radical location of sexual difference, while still remaining *within the framework of our patrilineal class-structured, capitalist societies,* is above all also attacking a fundamental discovery of Judaism that lies in the separation of the sexes and in their incompatability: in castration if you like—the support of monotheism and the source of its eroticism.[29]

If religious language is gone from the world, this symbolic economy exists in more deeply suppressed, but nonetheless real, forms, not only in language but also in politics and subjectivity. In fact, one wonders if monotheistic ordering is more, instead of less, repressive when it has lost its explicit religious expression. Take, for instance, the separation of the public and private spheres upon which bourgeois capitalism depends. Bourgeois patriarchy, in a manner similar to other forms of patriarchy, requires the social role of a particular type of mothering and forms this politically through the radical separation of the public and the private. This division is covered with an ideology of natural roles, "natural" not due any longer to divine fiat but now caused by biological, sociological, psychological, and political necessity.[30] The private/public separation becomes the distinction upon which liberalism comes to rest. The public arena comes to represent not only individual rights and freedoms, but market exchange. This public, in order for the autonomous individual to exist, depends upon the private sphere in the form of women's place, not only to take care of procreation, but increasingly to absorb the private values that the bourgeoisie has to deny, things like friendship, tradition, religion, and kinship. Indeed, religion and tradition once used to justify women's inequality now find themselves placed with women in the private, supposedly nonnecessary, realm. The social-symbolic economy is now politically liberal, free from explicit arguments about God's rule, but operating implicitly with the same monotheistic ordering: the public and paternal rulers, the autonomous agents dividing and exchanging the world, independent in theory but dependent in reality upon the private realm, the realm of the maternal, the realm of birth, death, morality, nurturing, relationships, connections, and also the realm of religion, art, tradition, of otherness, transformation, connectedness, transcendence.

Subjectivity is determined in the symbolic economy via patrilineal and political systems that ensure the full humanity of the citizen. That is, bourgeois liberalism protects a particular subject, projected in terms of full humanity, protected by an ideology of equal rights, and dependent upon the patriarchal ordering of the public/private realm. When, in the United States, women wanted the vote, their arguments were articulated first in terms of women's potential to be a citizen, but what finally won the vote for women was an argument based on the idea of woman's special moral nature and habits of housecleaning.[31] It was women's duty to help clean up the mess of politics, or so claimed the suffragists in league with the temperance movement. Though women "won" the vote, the suffrage movement receded quickly and the cult of domestic women rose strongly.[32] There are many explanations of why, though the suffrage movement won the right to vote, it failed to make the broad changes promised by such a movement. Amid these varied arguments, it is necessary to recognize that the liberal suffragists' argument concerning the full humanity and equality of all persons carries with it an anthropological requirement of a repressed maternal space since the autonomous individual must have certain needs met in a repressed and hidden manner. In such a way, it can also be understood why suffrage could pass only as it appealed to deeply satisfying images of women as mother, but such images faded, or rather molded themselves into the domestic women of a rapidly industrializing society when the task was over. The suffragist with dustmop and scrub bucket in hand to clear up the drunken slovenliness of her society easily, and in great comfort, slid to the housewife with her new appliances of vacuum cleaners and washing machines to clean, day after day, the space of rest and respite.

A similar problem is present when feminist theologians argue for the full humanity of women or the equality of "individuals." Such language, such claims, are already based on categories built into the social-symbolic order in which individualism and equality exist in relation to the repressed connectedness of women represented in the social-symbolic order. To advocate the full humanity of women is to adhere to, if not to idolize, the very category that has been erected upon the oppression and mystification of women. The problem is not only the oppression of women, but the requirements of the terms of full humanity and the demands of anthropological language in the social-symbolic order which construct the identity of the subject upon the division of public and private realms, to say nothing of class divisions and the securing of competitive relations. This is not to oppose changing images and metaphors but it is to argue that these terms and images are problematic because of the presuppositions built into the economy of the social-symbolic order that dispose feminism to correct rather than to transform bourgeois liberalism.

At least one should entertain the contention that language, subjectivity, and politics follow, in the present situation, a patriarchal-monotheistic ordering, despite the absence of explicit allegiance to any language of God. Feminism, especially that of liberal egalitarianism, has failed to question this ordering, using instead the terms of modernity, especially in the theories of liberalism and humanism, to question the application and effects of modern discourse. But without pursuing ways to rend and renew the patriarchal-monotheistic ordering that pervades language, subjectivity, and politics, women will be forced either to be like men or to continue their traditional roles through a particular kind of mothering, even if let into the public space. In the third space of feminism, women claim a position from which to rend and renew the social-symbolic order through the pursuit of what has been, as "other," both a taboo and a precondition in the patriarchial-monotheistic ordering of modernity.

Speaking from the Margins

I have contended, throughout this book, that feminist theology, especially as represented by many of the books published in recent years, can be best understood as discourses of emancipatory transformation. Using a variety of genres, understanding the Scriptures as prototypes and not archetype, and affirming the reality and visions of women-church, feminist theology has started to claim its space as a radical critique of the rules and principles of the social-symbolic order and to locate resources for new ways of speaking of freedom and freely speaking. I have argued that, in this manner, feminist theology proclaims the

Word to and for the world, a Word now not as primal referent for monotheistic ordering but as perfectly open sign that blesses specificity, difference, solidarity, embodiment, anticipation, and transformation. This leads to understanding feminist theology in terms different from those of modern theology, describing feminist theologies as discourses that follow abductive logic and that concentrate on the aesthetic play of images in relation to the rhetorical practices of community. In addition, I have suggested that feminist theology must be understood not as a mere corrective in theology but as a reconstruction of theological symbols, practices, and orderings. But it is also important that feminist theology be clear about itself as discourses of emancipatory transformation, and that it become intentional about its discourses as neither corrections nor supplements to the social-symbolic order but as attempts to rend and renew the social-symbolic order.

This requires, of course, that any reflection on women begin not by securing an essence of experience or by trying to make women into something that they are not and cannot be, but by considering the position of women in the present social-symbolic order and likewise standing in this position to try to transform the social-symbolic order. It again must be emphasized that to describe women's marginality is to deny any claim about the essence of woman's subjectivity, to forego a quest for the identity of "woman" as a universal singular. To describe women's experience is not, in some ahistorical fashion, to define experience, unless the original meaning of define is followed which, as Kenneth Burke notes, means setting in relation to, finding a space for, positioning.[33] Furthermore, the positionality of woman must be considered dialectically in terms of the satisfaction it has offered for men and women as well as the destruction it has wrecked on men and women. There has been satisfaction attained in the social-symbolic order, even in the split between the private and the public: women, at least some women some of the time, have been real subjects, have loved and have experienced joy in and on the margins of the system. Refusal to consider the full range of women's experiences, their joys and sufferings, has resulted in the denial of the complexity of women's experience for it is this complexity and particularity that threaten not only a critique but also a transformation of modernity.[34] Although its excesses on the one hand and its outburst against patriarchy on the other may produce the impetus for critique and transformation, feminism must never overlook or deny the validity and reality of the lives of women in this age and in the past.

To further, then, the proclamation of emancipatory transformation, feminism—in the power of the Word, the vision of the Scriptures, and formation of community—must pursue the richness of women's marginality to push against the ordering of language, subjectivity, and politics and to find new images, ways, forms, expressions of language, subjectivity, and politics. Three characteristics of women's marginality may be identified to illustrate present and possible resources for the rending and renewing of the social-symbolic order: (1) the oppression of women to repress what might threaten the social-symbolic order, (2) the religious piety of women in the day-to-day practices in the private realm, and (3) a subjectivity marked by a spatiality of containment and adornment and a temporality characterized as cyclical and cosmic.

First, women are oppressed, denied access to the social-symbolic order, described as sex objects or nonsexual, silenced both legally and culturally. Corrective efforts only seem to make Eve's fate worse: women in the work force are relegated by and large to jobs of feeding, typing, filing, nursing, social work, and taking care of others. This exclusion from so-called "fulfilling" work in the public realm is itself not the only problem, though in the sphere of productive relations it is usually the first one addressed. But women are also oppressed by being at the physical disposal of men in the various forms of patriarchy through the binding of feet, the raping in war and daily living, the medical practices that mutilate women's bodies and emotions. Women are denied the power of naming, for among other things, the problem of what to do with one's surname is seemingly impossible: if a woman marries, not to take her husband's name is to stay with the name of her father. Without discounting the physical and emotional suffering of women, it is also necessary to view the deep ambiguities in women's oppression: for while women have been oppressed, denied their potential, and forced into submission, they have also had relationships of love and respect with men as well as with women. Constituted through a set of relations deeply repressive to men and women, such relationships meet, negate, or even exceed women's repressed desires.[35] An analysis of women's oppression can begin by recognizing women as consigned the role of the "other" within the social-symbolic order. As consigned the role of "other" women have been denied as full human beings, to use the phrase common to humanism, and, at the same time, repressed as being not fully human, controlled, mastered, kept in place. Women are oppressed at the margins of psychic and political life for what *woman* represents: the bodily figuration of knowledge, the power of desire, the promise of birth and death, the constant resignification beyond all order.

From this locus that is not subsumed under the social-symbolic order's terms of equality and autonomous right, critique and transformation must be offered, critique and transformation that will not depend on the notion of a unique essence expressed in all women. This critique must be particular, speaking from situations of oppression, but must also be complex, carefully tracing the interrelations between productive and reproductive relations. Elizabeth Cady Stanton, the philosopher of the suffrage movement, called for critiques that would understand the thoroughness of patriarchy while also working for legal, economic, ecclesial, and political reforms. Cady Stanton argued that every invidious distinction of sex must be discussed, since woman's bondage was limited to no single issue but was structured through society in customs, language, laws, religion, and even personal relationships.[36] Though Cady Stanton's solution was the epitome of liberal egalitarianism, based on a woman's right to be an individual and a citizen, her writings offer a vision of both a thorough and a specific critique from the margins. So, too, must resistance and transformation begin with such critiques, and in expressing the marginality of women explore new assumptions for politics that emphasize difference and specificity, and new forms of subjectivity that recognize both the otherness and the connectedness within women.

On these margins, at the bottom of the hierarchical system of order, women, except in the exceptional cases of female mystics, cannot transcend to God or, in modernity, fully re-present God. How can woman, being not and not-being, have the "limit experiences" that the religious order requires, when women are already and always outside the limits? How can women, other and divided, speak of God in the gathered assembly? Yet women have had, and continue to have, religious experiences, though such experiences seem to be different than those of most men. Women's religious practices, so rarely talked about in great religious and theological literature, are lived out in the realm of the private, composed of duty, nurturing, preparing, waiting, taking care—the religiosity of the domestic.[37] And, as religion has joined women in the margins of modernity, in the realm of the private, in the so-called nonessential realm, women's religiosity comes to look more and more intuitive of religion itself.

Again, this position should be looked at in all its ambiguities: on the one hand, women's religious practices are channeled through a repressive religious ideology that uses the language and the structuring of ultimate values to keep women in their place: God ordered Eve's punishment and Paul assured her sentence. Yet, on these margins the importance of women's religious practices should not be ignored: women have had a place of residency with God in the day-to-day living out of reproductive systems, in the caring for wounded, the birthing of children, the feeding of souls and bodies. Many women have found, and find today, these practices deeply satisfying, and in the midst of day-to-day existence neither need nor desire limit experiences, ultimate concerns, or break-in interruptions of God to dwell with the Spirit. Many, though by no means all, women have found, and continue to find, in their religious-political duty an expression of their religiosity. Of course this is constituted by the social-symbolic order: women are to be loving, caring, quiet, behind the scenes—and, alternately, some women have found these religious practices too much of a burden, too empty, too repressive, and too violent.

From this position, questions can be raised on a number of levels, including the very definition of religion in modernity. Has not religion, at least in mainline Protestant and Catholic traditions, sought to secure the identity of the bourgeois subject? Catholics have joined Protestants in forcing religion into a subjectivity primarily existentially and/or transcendentally determined. Both theologically and sociologically, religion has been understood as giving meaning to individuals on the one hand, and providing coherence to social unity on the other. In the first instance, religion takes care of the limits of bourgeois existence—that which the social-symbolic order denies, represses, or forgets—describing and proscribing moments of transcendence from this order through terms such as awe, *mysterium tremendum et fascinans,* ultimacy in individual existence. In the second instance, religion is "mere" rhetoric, a leftover ideology appealing to social unity. But in the piety of many women, religious experience is neither isolated in unconnected special experiences nor rigidified in assertions of social unity, but practiced in the daily connections of life. Many women have found satisfaction in expressing their piety and knowledge of God in the language of caring for and being with rather than *mysterium tremendum et fascinans,* wholly other and ultimate concern. The nexus of religious experiences, at least for many women, is in and through relationships, friends, families, memories of the dead. Could the vision of God today—in a day desperate for care, sustenance, relationality, and physicality—come from a woman's day-to-day walk with her God?

It is also this sojourn, however briefly, into women's religious practices, that leads us to the third characteristic of women's positionality and of women's marginality to the social-symbolic order: the subjectivity of women's space and time. To live in the world is to live in space and time; the philosophers define it, the poets sing it, the artists portray it, we inhabit it. Women, put on the margins as "other," denied in importance and in worth and value, yet absolutely necessary, have a space that is, in one sense, "pre-public": the private realm. Today many women occupy both the space of the public and the space of the private: work, travel, and public history, alongside dwelling, staying, and contained environment—all expressed in discourses of the superwoman. This may prove impossible to maintain, and perhaps the realms will fade, or take on different signification; perhaps women will have to bend completely to the controlling complicity of the public. But the positionality of the space, in the present, remains for women both through a space of containment and through the adornment of that space. Woman's place in the home is surely an oppressive space, confining women to a building that has no public access, no public gathering, no opportunities to form public relationships or enjoy public activities. In America the feminist movement of the 1960s owes a great debt to Betty Friedan's *The Feminine Mystique,* which confronts the confined space for women in modern suburbia.[38] Yet what characterizes this space constructively is that the necessary preconditions of life, the very materiality of life are found here: eating, sleeping, the place of celebration and sorrow, of pride and anguish. These are not seen as valuable or necessary to the social-symbolic order but are, like woman herself, the presuppositions of all life. Women's space is also a "retreat" for her family from the world, and while this is deeply ambiguous, forcing women into violent modes of caretaking and nurturing, it has been a space out of the public and, in recent years, away from productive relations, and thus a space potentially against and in excess of the public, a place where basic needs are met and *jouissance,* "totality of enjoyment or ecstasy," occurs.

Central to women's space, not only the space she occupies but the space she inhabits with her body, is adornment, beauty. The oppressive and repressive aspects of this spatiality, in terms of the social-symbolic order narrowly defining beauty, must be emphasized. That women must look a certain way, preferably young and slightly silly, or fix their homes in fashion-plate antiseptic boredom, is simply more confirmation of the manipulation of modern psychic destruction. But, it can also be looked at in a different fashion, with adornment as the quest to beautify space and hence the dwelling of physical life, in various ways, through changes in color, in texture, in style. None of this, until manipulated by a productive system destructive of physicality, is necessarily proof of one's goodness or even suggestive of a telos in history but rather testifies to life itself merely for the sake of physical, sensual feeling. The space of woman on the borders of the order surrounds and makes adornment possible: in precondition and in retreat, in ongoing survival is the *jouissance* of beauty, pleasure, desire for feeling, releasing, being—all of which the social-symbolic order is both afraid of and must try to master.

Women's subjectivity is also marked by that which is outside the social-symbolic order: time of cycle, rhythm, and birth, time of physical pain and pleasure that will not conform always to schedules and timetables. The temporality of the maternal, the temporality in which we all begin our lives, is marked by a dual character, cyclical and cosmic, both of which exist outside the linear time of the social-symbolic order and have been consigned to women's subjectivity.[39] Cyclical time is the temporality one thinks of with "nature": fertilization, gestation, birth; one cannot here rise above or order the process, one must live with the rhythms of this time. This is time of connection and time that flows, from one cycle to the next, natural procession, life without end. Cosmic time, of a monumental nature, is also represented in the temporality of maternality, the temporality that explodes space and time, in every birth, begins. Cosmic time is the possibility of the splitting of one subject from another, stretching into infinity, infinite hope, infinite separation.

The temporality of women provides a place of critique for the oppressiveness of linear time: time which posits a cause-effect progressive movement from one thought to the next, from one event to the next, from one word to the next. Time of cycle and cosmos provides the precondition for living in time as order and progress: time must, after all, both begin and exist in a fashion that needs to be ordered. But time as cycle and cosmos exceeds the limits of linear time by living in the expansion and explosion of time as well as in the chaos and emptiness of time. To speak from this temporality, mindful of how the ambiguities have forced women to wait patiently in dreary monotony, may be to speak of a God who is experienced in change and rupture, in creative acts, in nature, in connections, in ways of life not ordered through modernity as the providence of God.

It is within the multivalency of time and space in women's subjectivity that feminism may question the modern ordering of subjectivity, language, and politics. Feminism may express alternatives, albeit ones marked with ambiguities, but ones that are both prior to and in excess of the social-symbolic ordering of modernity. From this place feminism questions the constant emphasis on identity and sameness at the expense of difference and specificity. For though "woman" is postulated as different in order to maintain the identity and equality of men, she lives in the difference and specificity in the ongoing relationality of women and women, women and children, women and nature, women and creation, women and beauty. Yet in this difference is also the abyss that means one is never to be completely united, never to experience connectedness of the sojourn or continual transformation within subjectivity, language, and politics. It is possible to imagine a new relation to the body and to God, to creation and redemption, to law and to grace, not from a subjectivity that must destroy everything in its path to maintain and establish its identity, but from a subjectivity, a language, and a politics that desires and embraces otherness, multiplicity, and difference.

Such a subjectivity, language, and politics stressing difference and specificity might also emphasize mutuality and corporality in a new vision of emancipatory transformation. Traditionally *mutuality* connotes being in relationship to God and others and traditionally this has been organized in women's ability to care and to nurture. But it has been both materially repressed and idealistically elevated. Mutuality has been separated from desire in the biological, sociological, and psychological arguments for a particular practice of mothering, while desire has been elevated idealistically in various visions of ultimate signification. Augustine, to take one example, separated mutuality from desire to elevate the latter to the nature of the spiritual journey, the desire that never rests until in God. From the margins women must join in their speech and practices the relations of mutuality and desire: the desire that knows constant resignification, the desire that is the very longing in mutuality that is never finally ruled in obedience and duty, never named or explained totally in symbolic ordering. This mutuality exists in women's physical connectedness, linguistic practices, and cultural traditions; it does not make all women the same nor does it set women as some collective body totally apart. It is a mutuality that makes possible love and freedom, and vice versa, in the ever transformative reality of subjectivity, language, and politics.

Corporality—love of body, earth, sensuality, materiality in the margins—has been fatefully configured as sinful and repressed, in the connection of corporality and death. There is some hidden wisdom in the paranoia of this ordering, for it is finally women's bodies that get torn in separation, women's bodies that die to live and live to die. Maternality may be one value of this discourse, though by no means the only source.[40] Maternality suggests the relationship among bodies, otherness, subjectivity, and perhaps even God. Love gives new birth, exceeding always the regulation and requirements of moral order. Luther's notion of justification includes, in this sense, a poetics of the maternal: Luther could not win in the contest with the law of the Father, and thus he is reborn through justification: love which bears without requirement, without order, without duty.[41] Love comes unconditionally and gives new birth through death of the one, in the torn apartness of one who gives birth and the one who is born. Corporality must not be the "otherness" that has to be disciplined, mastered, raped, or controlled. The link between nature and women in the social-symbolic order has been used to plunder, to exploit, to deny the goodness of creation, of touch, of a diffuse centeredness that is not related to a fixed identity of the I. But here, in the margins, the I is simply a marker, constantly bridging a gap in the corporality of earth, body, nature, language, culture, and history. In a proclamation of emancipatory transformation, corporality involves not only an ethics of eco/justice but a poetics of nature, a nature which is not merely given, neutral, or natural, but is constantly pushing against the order, transforming that very order.[42]

It is the positionality of women, the religious practices of daily connections, women's time and space—adornment, containment, cyclical, cosmic—that serve as loci for the possibility of a new subjectivity, new linguistic practices, perhaps, even a new politics. As has been suggested already, the very constitution of a particular way of being in time and space, of configuring history, and of ordering language leads to an identity of the self that is protected and procured only through the violent destruction of life, both the life of the other and the other life that is always within. Thus the critique, and proclamation as a critique, does not try to find a new identity of the subject, a new revised humanism in which the self or subject is assured prior to language and politics. This identity of the self (which has been labeled a narcissistic pattern) is a misrecognition that Christianity, in the long context of its theology in which the subject is decentered in relation to God, must oppose. For this misrecognition is instantiated through oppressive and repressive practices toward the "others" of history, practices concerning the physical, psychological, and spiritual conditions put onto women's bodies. From the margins of women's position, as dangerous as this may be, persuasive discourse first proclaims the judgment against the idolatry of the self whose independence depends upon the materiality of the "others" of history.

In this questioning and judgment, in this critique and uncovering, in the marginality that both grounds and pushes against the murderous intent of language which constantly enforces an ahistorical a priori self, proclamation can speak of an emancipatory transformation in the constant decentering and resignification of self, God, world, and community. In this way to proclaim the Word to and for the world is not to claim a secure end, a final subject, a clear language, a determined politics, but precisely to open up the possibilities to live and move in the complexities, ambiguities, and richness of language, subjectivity, and politics. It is to speak forth of continual union and separation, incarnation and diffusion, in the emancipatory process of new life that both is and is to come.

Conclusion

Proclamation is given to the world, the Word for the world, God and world together. The church is not created for fellowship, continued support, spiritual nourishment or even social service; rather, the church is called to proclaim, to give to the world news of emancipatory transformation. There is no one way to do this, no one long progression of the history of the Word with an origin and an end. The Spirit blows and roots where it will. Today proclamation must be a critique and transformation of the social-symbolic order, a critique and transformation not only of the functions and effects of this order but also of its basic ordering, its support and foundations in language, subjectivity, and politics.

This is an enormous task. It will not be, of course, the sole duty of the church and certainly not the unique privilege of Christianity to transform the social-symbolic order! Indeed, as should be clear by now,

Christianity must undergo, in proclaiming Word to and with the world, its own thorough transformation, one in which Christianity's complicity with the modern order is questioned and uncovered. As long as Jesus is imaged as a kerygmatic Lord who comes to those who sit in church on Sunday morning or as a new being which utters, often anonymously, a yes to bourgeois existence, as long as the sermon's purpose is primarily to feed the individual, as long as the time and space of God is ordered only through the clock, Christianity has little to say to the world. Yet perhaps it is precisely in speaking, in questioning the ordering and the discursive and nondiscursive practices of modernity that Christianity will itself be transformed, calling into question its control as well as its play of tradition, Gospel, Spirit, and community. The task is enormous, for not only does it call into question the order, but it requires a radical reformation of Christianity, one in which God, manifest in the margins, is listened to, lived with, adored.

The task would become too enormous were it not for the magnitude of Spirit already present in the margins and ambiguities of language, subjectivity, and politics; enormous, not only because of the transformation it creates in Christianity, but because of the breadth and depth of the critique and the way that critique must be accomplished. The critique of the way things are must include a critique of systems and structures, including ongoing criticism of economic, legal, educational, and governmental institutions. It must question the formation and application of ideas and theories, continuing the inclusion of ideology critique in Christianity and theology. But the critique of proclamation must push farther and deeper to criticize the ordering, assumptions, contracts, configurations, and anonymous rules of the dominant practices that run through language, subjectivity, and politics. What has been termed a monotheistic ordering—expressed in the self-referentiality of language, the narcissistic patterning of the autonomous individual, the self-preservation of the state—must be uncovered and resisted. Until this ordering is called into question, exposed in its constant loyalty to keeping things the same, its obedience to the royal rules of division and subjection, any critique will necessarily function as a corrective to the system. It is no longer enough to assert, under the rules of modernity's monotheism, the inclusion of the marginal: they are, at best, included only if they obey monotheistic practices as representatives of autonomy, identity, self-referentiality. Rather, the policies of inclusion and exclusion, the rules of formation and expulsion, the figurations of public and private as forms of the dominant ordering must be uncovered. Only if it is possible to denounce the continual preferences, commandments, assumptions, and images of modernity's ordering, is it possible to announce transformation.

The possibility of a proclamation of God's Word to and for the world begins by exposing, interrupting, and pushing against the rules and constructs that operate in similar fashion in language, subjectivity, and politics. In relation to language, proclamation must call into question the self-referentiality of language, and the correspondence of language with authorial intention, analytic procedures, and univocal rules. Language must be constituted as multivocal, open, practical, anticipatory: rich, embodied, full of connections and of differences. While language in modernity reflects a monotheistic ordering, in feminist proclamation language constitutes an open possibility for transformation.[43]

Subjectivity, the limits and possibilities of what a human subject is allowed to be and to experience, which in modernity has been constructed primarily by and for male subjects, must be resisted in its autonomous, narcissistic patterning wherein only that which reflects the self is desired, a desire that can never be satisfied. I have suggested that women's space and time offer possibilities for a transforming vision of subjectivity: adornment rather than narcissism, containment rather than mastery, beauty rather than control, cycle and cosmos rather than lineality and progression. Within its visions, histories, and stories, Christianity has long been concerned with images of human subjectivity: it today may provide resources for the views of multiple subjectivity and a subjectivity that is not contained within a preordained identity but one that is always, to use the classic phrase, on a journey unto God.[44]

Finally, feminist discourses of proclamation must address the monotheistic ordering in politics, especially the politics of self-preservation and bureaucratic management. Any critique that looks at the determination of the relation between the sexes and the physical control of time, space, and relation to nature is political, as is any critique looking at institutional practices and cultural values, images, and worldviews. The critique of politics necessarily includes both language and subjectivity. Yet it must also today speak directly of a renewed citizenship and participation in government, of an openness and solidarity with the many, of peace and justice that is, in a very historical sense, universal and free for all.[45] The critique of politics must move away from setting up associative practices through the autonomous rules of a social contract toward the ongoing formation of habits and shared practices in communities which nurture, above all else, the ability to live together, to embrace specificity and difference, to work and play for mutual enrichment.

As mentioned already, there is no one method or theory that can accomplish the needed transformation. There are, instead, insights and strategies that arise out of the margins that may allow for new possibilities and visions. The viewing of the social-symbolic order from the position of marginality to the order examines the workings and nonworkings of the ordering. No claim to see perfectly or totally is advocated, but in the questions and uncovering of particular practices and basic orderings new possibilities arise. Though the marginality of women has provided the space to offer critique and transformation in this book, other positions with different types of perspectives are needed. The persuasiveness of emancipatory transformation will be gained not by adopting one position or reifying one theory, but, at least in these in-between times, by standing in solidarity where the Spirit moves in questions, ruptures, excesses, and changes.

Conceived in this way, feminist theology is good news, good news to the desperate world, to the hungry masses, to desiring individuals, to the diseased planet. It is good news for all, because, as this book has tried to demonstrate, the present social-symbolic order works for no one. The present order has helped create the crisis of mere survival for many of the world's people and for the physical earth itself. The threat of nuclear annihilation, of poverty and illness, of injustice and oppression are related to the ordering of preservation, identity, control, and autonomy that operates insidiously in modernity through how modernity organizes time and space (the lineality of history, the mastery of frontiers), to how modernity reads and thus controls meaning (the powerful reader knows the authorial intent and thus the real meaning), the management of politics (who's really responsible for dropping all the bombs since the soldier just does his job?). Those who supposedly reap the benefits of modernity, the bourgeoisie, are beset with psychic destructiveness, depression, drugs, alcohol, consumerism. The bourgeoisie use most of the world's resources in gluttony, but without connection, embodiment, solidarity, and anticipation they have no satisfaction, only the discomfort of overwhelmed senses.

The proclamatory discourses of Word and world will be more than a mere no to the social-symbolic order, though they will offer a no to the continuing perpetuation of modernity's murderous effects. Rather, transformations occur in departures from and reformulations of ideas, theories, traditions, words, cultural forms, and economic practices; in seeing differently feminism finds no totally new way of being and doing, as if a magic city from above could appear, but rather in the wandering and movement of a sojourn in the wilderness, feminism can discover and create new ways of dwelling. Thus proclamation has, for the present, no total interpretations, no new social-symbolic orderings, but rather revolution and reformation that may emerge, at present in piecemeal and partial fashion, as the Spirit erupts, questions, looks again, shifts. Indeed new forms of language, subjectivity, and politics in which otherness is celebrated rather than cast on others as taboo, comes out of the gaps and margins but also arises amid the dissolving possibilities of an order that can no longer be maintained. The hope is not that feminism can give all the answers but that feminism can hold fast to tracing the possibilities of questioning anew.

NOTES

Epigraph on pp. vi-vii: Marge Piercy, "For Strong Women," in *The Moon Is Always Female* (New York: Knopf, 1986), pp. 56–57.

Introduction

Epigraphs: Kenneth Burke, "The Poetic Motive," *The Hudson Review* (Spring 1958), quoted in his *The Rhetoric of Religion: Studies in Logology* (Berkeley and Los Angeles: University of California Press, 1970), p. 15; Nelle Morton, *The Journey Is Home* (Boston: Beacon Press, 1985), p. 87.

1. Current feminist theory, in general, questions the ability of dominant systems of thought to attend to feminist concerns. Thus most feminist theory centers on the reconstruction of theory and practice from a feminist perspective. Elaine Showalter summarizes the current trend in feminist theory in the following manner: "the feminist obsession with correcting, modifying, supplementing, revising, humanizing, or even attacking male critical theory keeps us dependent upon it and retards our progress in solving our own theoretical problems. What I mean here by 'male critical theory' is a concept of creativity, literary history, or literary interpretation based entirely on male experience and put forward as universal. So long as we look to androcentric models for our most basic principles—even if we revise them by adding the feminist frame of reference—we are learning nothing new" ("Feminist Criticism in the Wilderness," *Critical Inquiry* 8 [1981]: 183). Though this theme has captured the attention of a wide variety of feminist thinkers, it is also necessary to observe that feminist writing has almost always hinted that this might be the case. See, for instance, Valerie Saiving, "The Human Situation: A Feminine View," in *Womanspirit Rising: A Feminist Reader in Religion*, ed. Carol P. Christ and Judith Plaskow (San Francisco: Harper & Row, 1970), p. 25.

2. Helene Cixous, "Sorties," in *New French Feminisms: An Anthology*, ed. Elaine Marks and Isabelle de Courtivron (New York: Schocken, 1981), p. 91. At least implicitly, Cixous hints of the religious nature of this ordering of logocentrism and phallocentrism: "The challenging of this solidarity of logocentrism and phallocentrism has today become insistent enough—the bringing to light of the fate which has been imposed upon woman, of her burial—to threaten the stability of the masculine edifice which passed itself off as eternal-natural; by bringing forth from the world of femininity reflections, hypotheses which are

necessarily ruinous for the bastion which still holds the authority. What would become of logocentrism, of the great philosophical systems, of world order in general if the rock upon which they founded their church was to crumble?" Cixous projects a new vision once this ordering fails: "Then all the stories would have to be told differently, the future would be incalculable, the historical forces would, will, change hands, bodies, another thinking as yet not thinkable will transform the functioning of all society. Well, we are living through this very period when the conceptual foundation of a millennial culture is in process of being undermined by millions of a species of mole as yet not recognizable" (pp. 92–93).

3. Deborah Cameron, *Feminism and Linguistic Theory* (London: Macmillan, 1985), pp. 155–56.

4. Carolyn G. Heilbrun, *Writing a Woman's Life* (New York: Norton, 1988), p. 18.

5. Such questioning and questing by feminists is still interpreted by some male critics as merely trying to reverse the order—and thus place women "on the top," so to speak. In theology this is usually followed by an invocation of Neibuhrian realism to warn that power always corrupts. The point of feminism, however, is to transform the ordering itself, not to substitute for or correct the ordering. When feminism questions the basic ordering principles of modernity (and, in the case of this book, of Christianity), then we may see the wisdom of Virginia Woolf's observation, "Towards the end of the eighteenth century a change came about which, if I were re-writing history, I should describe more fully and think of greater importance than the Crusades or the Wars of the Roses. The middle-class woman began to write" (*A Room of One's Own* [New York: Harcourt, 1929], p. 68). Though by no means limited to middle-class women, Woolf's insight underscores that by writing women question (and threaten) the ordering itself. It is this ordering which many find so difficult to question or even to hear the questions of others, preferring instead to assume that the order, and its particular constructs of power, are "natural" or "inevitable."

6. For an excellent introduction to issues of language as a political activity in relation to feminism, see Chris Weedon, *Feminist Practice and Poststructuralist Theory* (Oxford: Basil Blackwell, 1987); and for an excellent discussion of various perspectives on language and politics, see Fred R. Dallymar, *Language and Politics: Why Does Language Matter to Political Philosophy?* (Notre Dame, IN: University of Notre Dame Press, 1984).

7. By social-symbolic order I mean the way things are, the dominant practices and principles in language, subjectivity, and politics. The term symbolic order is used in some forms of poststructuralism; as Weedon defines the meaning of Lacan's use of the term "symbolic order," it is "the social and cultural order in which we live our lives as conscious, gendered subjects. It is structured by language and the laws and social institutions which language guarantees" (*Feminist Practice and Poststructuralist Theory*, p. 52). As I explain in the first chapter, I use the term "order" to draw attention to the hidden rules, the anonymous principles and the unquestioned presuppositions that run through our subjectiv-

ity, language and politics. But I use the terms "social" and "symbolic" to emphasize that these presuppositions and rules are prior to the individual (though not completely determinative) and always symbolic (endowed with meaning by human action). For a pragmatist reading of the social-symbolic, see Hans Joas, *G. H. Mead: A Contemporary Re-examination of his Thought,* trans. Raymond Meyer (Cambridge: MIT Press, 1985).

8. I understand this work to be what Francis Schüssler Fiorenza calls a hermeneutical reconstruction, an interpretation but one that critically judges what constitutes Christian vision and identity. See Francis Schüssler Fiorenza, *Foundational Theology: Jesus and the Church* (New York: Crossroad, 1984), especially pp. 285–310.

9. This is one of Karl Rahner's contributions to Vatican II. See, for instance, *Lumen gentium.*

10. For example, see Gustavo Gutiérrez, *A Theology of Liberation: History, Politics and Salvation,* ed. and trans. Sister Caridad Inda and John Eagleson (Maryknoll, NY: Orbis, 1973), p. 260.

11. One may recall Paul Tillich's notion of the material norm of theology which provides the criterion to which sources and experience are subjected. The material norm is always specific to the historical situation, as Tillich states: "While the norm for the early Greek church was the liberation of finite man from death and error by the incarnation of immortal life and eternal truth, for the Roman church it was salvation from guilt and disruption by the actual and sacramental sacrifice of the God-man. For modern Protestantism it was the picture of the 'synoptic' Jesus, representing the personal and social ideal of human existence; and for recent Protestantism it has been the prophetic message of the Kingdom of God in the Old and New Testaments" (*Systematic Theology,* 3 vols. [Chicago: University of Chicago Press, 1951], 1: 47–48). Note that for Tillich the material norm is related to the formal norm—which he understands to be that of a hierarchy of authorities—and thus represents the norm for theology "proper," the dominant theology espoused by the church of that day.

12. Richard Fox, *Reinhold Niebuhr: A Biography* (New York: Pantheon, 1985).

13. This seems especially clear to me in Calvin due both to theological warrants in which the human being is created to be in relationship to God and in terms of philosophical warrants by Calvin's use of rhetoric in the conception of theology. For the theological warrants entailed, see B. A. Gerrish, *The Old Protestantism and the New: Essays on the Reformation Heritage* (Chicago: University of Chicago Press, 1982), pp. 150–59. For the role of rhetoric in Calvin's thought, see David Willis, "Rhetoric and Responsibility in Calvin's Theology," in *The Context of Contemporary Theology: Essays in Honor of Paul Lehmann,* ed. A. J. McKelway and E. D. Willis (Atlanta: John Knox Press, 1974), and William J. Bouwsma, *John Calvin: A Sixteenth Century Portrait* (New York and Oxford: Oxford University Press, 1988).

14. Tillich, *Systematic Theology* 1:158. See also Paul Ricoeur, "Manifestation and Proclamation," *The Journal of Blaisdell Institute* 12 (Winter 1978): 13–35, and David Tracy, *The Analogical Imagination: Christian Theology and the Culture of Pluralism* (New York: Crossroad, 1981), pp. 202–18.

15. For an excellent understanding of what Luther and Calvin meant by a sacramental notion of the Word, see Gerrish, *The Old Protestantism and the New,* p. 66.

16. Jürgen Moltmann, *The Crucified God: The Cross of Christ as the Foundation and Criticism of Christian Theology,* trans. R. A. Wilson and John Bowden (New York: Harper & Row, 1973), pp. 7–28. One contemporary theology that might be considered a theology of the Word is Eberhard Jüngel, *God as the Mystery of the World: On the Foundation of the Theology of the Crucified One in the Dispute between Theism and Atheism,* trans. Darrell L. Guder (Grand Rapids, MI: Eerdmans, 1983).

17. Moltmann, *The Crucified God,* pp. 8–18. It is interesting to note that liberation theologies seem to have far more relevance to the broader society than most other forms of theology. Indeed, relevance in theology bears a relationship to the authority of theology in addressing contemporary issues; see Rebecca S. Chopp, "Theological Persuasion: Rhetoric, Warrants and Suffering," in *Worldviews and Warrants: Plurality and Authority in Theology,* ed. William Schweiker and Per M. Anderson (Lanham, MD: University Press of America, 1987), pp. 17–31.

18. See, for example, Karl Barth, *Church Dogmatics,* vol. 1, pt. 1, trans. G. T. Thompson (New York: Charles Scribner's Sons, 1936); idem, *The Word of God and the Word of Man,* trans. Douglas Horton (New York: Pilgrim Press, 1928); Rudolf Bultmann, *Faith and Understanding* (New York: Harper & Row, 1969); Gerhard Ebeling, *Word and Faith,* trans. James W. Leitch (Philadelphia: Fortress Press, 1963); idem, *Theology and Proclamation,* trans. John Riches (Philadelphia: Fortress Press, 1966); and Ernst Fuchs, *Hermeneutik* (Bad Cannstatt: Mullerschon, 1958).

19. For an important discussion of the notions of communicative action and solidarity, see Helmut Peukert, *Science, Action and Fundamental Theology: Toward a Theology of Communicative Action,* trans. James Bohman (Cambridge: MIT Press, 1984). Though I have questions about Peukert's communicative action approach, his readings are interesting and provocative. Indeed, one could only wish that his closing lines prove true: "An elementary experience seems to lie at the root of modern attempts to develop theories of intersubjectivity, society, and history. To speak unreservedly, it is the constitutive experience of a humanity that sees itself as emerging from evolution to consciousness and reflectivity. The universal communication community of these beings emerging from evolution and seeking mutual understanding demands its own sort of solidarity. . . . In the face of the Biblical tradition, the question of this solidarity must be put even more radically. Then it becomes the question of a reality that makes this solidarity possible, even in the face of the annihilation of the other in death" (p. 245).

20. A good example of how this kind of question is implicit in feminism can be found in Theresa De Lauretis, *Alice Doesn't: Feminism, Semiotics, Cinema* (Bloomington: Indiana University Press, 1982).

21. These terms, it seems to me, are what Margaret Farley calls central convictions "shared at least by large groups of feminists," and are certainly terms

present in contemporary feminist poetry and prose. The terms I list are expanded beyond Farley's set, which, in my judgement, seem to be terms gleaned from liberal feminism and not those of the kind of transformist feminism advocated in this text. See Margaret Farley, "Feminist Consciousness and Scripture," in *Feminist Interpretation of the Bible*, ed. Letty M. Russell (Philadelphia: Westminster Press, 1985), pp. 41–45.

22. The reconstructive method of this book employs semiotics, pragmatism, and rhetoric in addition to hermeneutics to address language as a political activity. Semiotics is used to address the signifying aspects of language and its poetic and revolutionary potential. Pragmatism is used to address the logic and status of discourse, and to remove it from any foundationalist claims. Rhetoric is used to draw attention to the historical character of language, including its purposive character.

23. See Elisabeth Schüssler Fiorenza, *In Memory of Her: A Feminist Theological Reconstruction of Christian Origins* (New York: Crossroad, 1983), especially pp. 26–36, and *Bread Not Stone: The Challenge of Feminist Biblical Interpretation* (Boston: Beacon Press, 1984), pp. 9–11.

24. Kenneth Burke says, "Hence, instead of considering it our task to 'dispose of' any ambiguity by merely disclosing the fact that it is an ambiguity, we rather consider it our task to study and clarify the *resources* of ambiguity. For in the course of this work, we shall deal with many kinds of *transformation*—and it is in the areas of ambiguity that transformations take place; in fact, without such areas, transformation would be impossible" (*A Grammar of Motives* [Berkeley and Los Angeles: University of California Press, 1969], p. xix). For an interesting and important reading about the loss of the capacity to deal with ambiguity in modernity, see Donald N. Levine, *The Flight from Ambiguity: Essays in Social and Cultural Theory* (Chicago: University of Chicago Press, 1985). For a treatment of ambiguity as a theological issue, see David Tracy, *Plurality and Ambiguity: Hermeneutics, Religion, Hope* (San Francisco: Harper & Row, 1987).

Chapter 1: Proclamation, Women, and the Word

Epigraph: Patricia Yaeger, *Honey-Mad Women: Emancipatory Strategies in Women's Writing* (New York: Columbia University Press, 1988), pp. 28–29.

1. In recent years, German political theology has interpreted middle-class existence, especially its consumerism, apathy, and individualism, as a form of enslavement or bondage. See, for instance, Johannes Baptist Metz, *Faith in History and Society: Toward a Practical Fundamental Theology*, trans. David Smith (New York: Seabury Press, 1980), and idem, *The Emergent Church: The Future of Christianity in a Postbourgeois World*, trans. Peter Mann (New York: Crossroad, 1981).

2. There are, of course, countless interpretations of modernity. Indeed, a crucial question for this "postmodern" age is how we interpret and understand the historical period of modernity. For an excellent place to begin, see Jürgen Habermas, *The Philosophical Discourses of Modernity: Twelve Lectures*, trans. Frederick Lawrence (Cambridge: MIT Press, 1987), and Paul De Man, *Blindness and Insight* (New York: Oxford University Press, 1971).

3. John Barth has suggested the defining characteristic of postmodernism is

that we do not try to pretend that the first half of this century did not happen: "It did happen: Freud and Einstein and two world wars and the Russian and sexual revolutions and automobiles and airplanes and telephones and radios and movies and urbanization, and now nuclear weaponry and television and microchip technology and the new feminism and the rest, and there's no going back to Tolstoy and Dickens & Co. except on nostalgia trips" ("The Literature of Replenishment," *Atlantic Monthly*, January 1980, p. 70). I am indebted to Alice A. Jardine, *Gynesis: Configurations of Woman and Modernity* (Ithaca, NY: Cornell University Press, 1985), p. 23, for the Barth quotation. For a broader description of postmodernism, see Ihab Hassan, *The Postmodern Turn: Essays in Postmodern Theory and Culture* (Columbus: Ohio State University Press, 1987). Postmodernism has also become a concern in theology; see Mark C. Taylor, *Erring: A Postmodern A/theology* (Chicago: University of Chicago Press, 1984); Sallie McFague, *Models of God: Theology for an Ecological, Nuclear Age* (Philadelphia: Fortress Press, 1987); and Peter C. Hodgson, *Revisioning the Church: Ecclesial Freedom in the New Paradigm* (Philadelphia: Fortress Press, 1988), and idem, *God and History: Shapes of Freedom* (Nashville: Abingdon Press, 1989).

4. It is necessary to employ both the words "emancipatory" and "transformation," emancipatory because the issues of the day have to do with freedom, in multiple and diverse ways, but transformation because only a changed ordering of our language, subjectivity, and politics will enable us to nurture new words and ways of freedom.

5. Since his groundbreaking *Theology of Liberation*, Gustavo Gutiérrez has maintained that the liberation movements in Latin America are a quest for new ways of being human. See also Matthew Lamb, *Solidarity with Victims: Toward a Theology of Social Transformation* (New York: Crossroad, 1982).

6. Indeed, from the beginnings of feminist theology there has been a wide variety of resources employed, questions asked, and procedures used. For an example of the variety within feminist theology in its early writings, see *Womanspirit Rising: A Feminist Reader in Religion*, ed. Christ and Plaskow, and the recent *Embodied Love: Sensuality and Relationship as Feminist Values*, ed. Paula M. Cooey, Sharon A. Farmer, and Mary Ellen Ross (San Francisco: Harper & Row, 1987), for a later example.

7. Among this list, Mary Daly is, by her own self-definition, no longer a theologian. Her famous work *Beyond God the Father: Toward a Philosophy of Women's Liberation* (Boston: Beacon Press, 1973) still works within theological constructs and is the book I am referring to as "rebirthing women's words in order to create a woman's space." Her books following *Beyond God the Father*, such as *Gyn/Ecology: The Metaethics of Radical Feminism* (Boston: Beacon Press, 1983) and *Pure Lust: Elemental Feminist Philosophy* (Boston: Beacon Press, 1984), also rebirth words to create woman's space but with no explicit concern for dialogue with Christian theology.

8. By language and discourse I mean to emphasize both the principles and rules that seem to make language work in a historical period, and the specific discourses operating within language at a given historical period. In my own

rhetorical approach, I am using the resources of structuralism, poststructuralism, materialism, semiotics, and phenomenology as ways of describing how language works in our particular situation. See Robert Detweiler, *Story, Sign and Self: Phenomenology and Structuralism as Literary-Critical Methods* (Philadelphia: Fortress Press, and Atlanta: Scholars Press, 1978); Terry Eagleton, *Literary Theory: An Introduction* (Minneapolis: University of Minnesota Press, 1983); *The Philosophy of Paul Ricoeur: An Anthology of His Work*, ed. Charles E. Reagan and David Stewart (Boston: Beacon Press, 1978); Paul Ricoeur, *Interpretation Theory* (Fort Worth: Texas Christian University Press, 1976); and Chris Weedon, *Feminist Practice and Poststructuralist Theory.*

9. Language is the only way we can *address* the world; any talk of the world is already constructed in language and discourse for as Heidegger observed, "Language is the house of being" (*Being and Time* [New York: Harper & Row, 1962], p. 145). Thinkers as diverse as Charles Sanders Peirce, Kenneth Burke, Jacques Derrida, Hans-Georg Gadamer, and Ludwig Wittgenstein, all in their own particular ways, have stressed the symbolic construct of reality through language. For two general accounts, see J. G. A. Pocock, *Politics, Language and Time: Essays on Political Thought and History* (New York: Atheneum, 1973), and Richard Harvey Brown, *Society as Text: Essays on Rhetoric, Reason and Reality* (Chicago: University of Chicago Press, 1987). Perhaps the writer that has received the most notice, thereby serving the useful purpose of calling attention, on a broader scale than just the confines of professional philosophers, to the historical and philosophical issues involved, has been Jacques Derrida in works such as *Dissemination*, trans. B. Johnson (Chicago: University of Chicago Press, 1981); *Glas* (Paris: Editions Galilee, 1974); *Of Grammatology*, trans. G. C. Spivak (Baltimore: Johns Hopkins University Press, 1976); *Margins of Philosophy*, trans. A. Bass (Chicago: University of Chicago Press, 1982); and *Writing and Difference*, trans. A. Bass (Chicago: University of Chicago Press, 1978).

10. See also De Lauretis, *Alice Doesn't*, p. 184.

11. See Weedon, *Feminist Practice and Poststructuralist Theory*, pp. 32–35, and Julia Kristeva, "About Chinese Women," in *The Kristeva Reader*, ed. Toril Moi (New York: Columbia University Press, 1986), pp. 139–58.

12. For an excellent analysis of consciousness raising, see Hester Eisenstein, *Contemporary Feminist Thought* (Boston: G. K. Hall, 1983).

13. See Weedon, *Feminist Practice and Poststructuralist Theory*, p. 37, and Michel Foucault, *Discipline and Punishment* (Harmondsworth: Penquin, 1979).

14. Detweiler, in his *Story, Sign, and Self*, provides a useful section on "Phenomenology and Structuralist Literary Criticism: Possibilities of Reconciliation," pp. 165–213. I am indebted to the work of Kenneth Burke and Charles Sanders Peirce for rhetorical and semiotic approaches to the structural and symbolic perspectives of language. For Burke, see especially *A Grammar of Motives, Permanence and Change* (Indianapolis: Bobbs-Merrill, 1965), and *Language as Symbolic Action: Essays on Life, Literature, and Method* (Los Angeles and Berkeley: University of California Press, 1966); for Charles Sanders Peirce, see *Collected Papers of Charles Sanders Peirce*, 6 vols., ed. Charles Hartshorne and Paul Weiss (Cambridge: Harvard University Press, 1960).

15. Hannah Arendt, *The Human Condition* (Chicago: University of Chicago, 1958).

16. Cameron, *Feminism and Linguistic Theory*, pp. 139–40.

17. Zillah R. Eisenstein, *The Radical Future of Liberal Feminism* (Boston: Northeastern University Press, 1981).

18. Toril Moi, *Sexual/Textual Politics: Feminist Literary Theory* (London: Methuen, 1985), p. 167.

19. Many French women writers refuse to use the term "feminist," since they see feminism as a movement coming out of humanist and liberal discourses. American feminists, however, use the term with little reservation perhaps because the term is more immediately connected to political action than to academic critique. For an excellent discussion of the relations between French and American feminism, see Jardine, *Gynesis*, pp. 13–28. My own concerns in this debate are that we must refuse to adhere to any "essence of women" position and that we accept the political agenda of feminism, including as part of that agenda issues of language and subjectivity. In many respects, I agree with Julia Kristeva when she says, "In the twentieth century, after suffering through fascism and revisionism, we should have learned that there can be no sociopolitical transformation without a transformation of subjects: in other words, in our relationship to social constraints, to pleasure, and more deeply, to language" "La femme, ce n'est jamais ca," an interview by "psychoanalysis and politics," in *Tel quel*, Autumn 1974, reprinted [trans. Marilyn A. August] in *New French Feminisms: An Anthology*, ed. Marks and Courtivron, p. 141).

20. Sharon Welch speaks of this in terms of her double identity as oppressor and oppressed, in *Communities of Resistance and Solidarity: A Feminist Theology of Liberation* (Maryknoll, NY: Orbis, 1985), p. ix.

21. Julia Kristeva speaks of the difficulty of grasping the power of destructive forces within the individual and society in our present situation, stating, "As horrible as the political and military cataclysms have been, and as much as they defy comprehension by their monstrous violence—concentration camps or the atomic bomb—the violently intense deflagration of psychic identity remains equally difficult to grasp" ("The Pain of Sorrow in the Modern World: The Works of Marguerite Duras," *PMLA* 102 [1987]: 138).

22. See Rebecca S. Chopp, "Feminism's Theological Pragmatics: A Social Naturalism of Women's Experience," *The Journal of Religion* 67 (1987): 239.

23. The idea of moving beyond Christianity was invoked in the first wave of feminism in the United States. See Elizabeth Cady Stanton, ed., *The Original Feminist Attack on the Bible: The Woman's Bible* (1895; New York: Arno Press, 1974), and Charlotte Perkins Gilman, *His Religion and Hers: A Study in the Faith of Our Fathers and the Work of Our Mothers* (London: Fisher, Anovin, 1924).

24. Many women have remarked that even as Christianity has oppressed them, they have heard in Christianity words of freedom. Elisabeth Schüssler Fiorenza, for instance, has observed: "Despite all masculine terminology of prayers, catechism, and liturgy, despite blatant patriarchal male spiritual guidance, my commitment to Christian faith and love first led me to question the feminine cultural role which parents, school and church had taught me to ac-

cept and to internalize. My vision of Christian life-style, responsibility, and community brought me to reject the culturally imposed role of women and not vice versa" ("Feminist Spirituality, Christian Identity, and Catholic Vision," in *Womanspirit Rising: A Feminist Reader in Religion*, ed. Christ and Plaskow, p. 137). I am indebted to the insights of Patricia Yaeger in *Honey-Mad Women* for the notion of emancipatory strategies in women's writings.

25. Rosemary Radford Ruether, *Sexism and God-Talk: Toward a Feminist Theology* (Boston: Beacon Press, 1983).

26. Ibid., "The Kenosis of the Father: A Feminist Midrash on the Gospel in Three Acts," pp. 1–11, and "Postscript: Woman/Body/Nature: The Icon of the Divine," pp. 259–66.

27. Elisabeth Schüssler Fiorenza, "The 'Quilting' of Women's History: Phoebe of Cenchreae," in *Embodied Love: Sensuality and Relationship as Feminist Values*, ed. Cooey, Farmer, and Ross, pp. 35–49.

28. Ibid., p. 35. The metaphor of quilting has become important for feminist studies. Elaine Showalter makes the distinction between "piecing" as the "sewing together of small fragments of fabric cut into geometric shapes, so that they form a pattern"; patchwork as "the joining of these design units into an overall design"; and quilting as the attaching of the assembled patches onto a stiff backing. Showalter comments: "Thus the process of making a patchwork quilt involves three separate stages of artistic composition, with analogies to language use first on the level of sentence, then in terms of the structure of a story or novel, and finally the images, motifs, or symbols—the 'figure in the carpet'—that unify a fictional work" ("Piecing and Writing," in *The Poetics of Gender*, ed. Nancy K. Miller [New York: Columbia University Press, 1986], p. 223). See also Radka Donnell-Vogt, "Memoir," in *Lives and Works: Talks with Women Artists*, ed. Lynn F. Miller and Sally S. Swenson (Metuchen, NJ: Scarecrow Press, 1961).

29. Elisabeth Schüssler Fiorenza, "The 'Quilting' of Women's History," p. 36.

30. Ibid.

31. Catherine Keller, *From a Broken Web: Separation, Sexism, and Self* (Boston: Beacon Press, 1986).

32. Elisabeth Schüssler Fiorenza, *Bread Not Stone*, p. 3.

33. Much of modern theology has tried to explain itself to the cultured despisers, or secularists. See Friedrich Schleiermacher, *On Religion: Speeches to Its Cultured Despisers* (New York: Harper & Row, 1965); Schubert Ogden, *The Reality of God* (New York: Harper & Row, 1966); and Karl Rahner, *Foundations of Christian Faith: An Introduction to the Idea of Christianity* (New York: Crossroad, 1978). For a criticism of this "progressive theology" and its concern for the nonbeliever instead of the nonperson, see Gustavo Gutiérrez, *The Power of the Poor in History*, trans. Robert R. Barr (Maryknoll, NY: Orbis, 1983), p. 93.

34. Kenneth Burke argues in *The Rhetoric of Religion* that we should explore the analogy between theology, "words about God," and logology, "words about words," because statements by theologians about God might be adapted for use about words. I am suggesting the reverse of Burke's project since God, in

Christianity, is understood and figured as Word, we may arrive at some new understanding of God and Word by considering how, in our time and day, words about words work. See Burke, *The Rhetoric of Religion,* pp. 1–42.

35. Ibid., p. 25.

36. It is in fact the case that many of the sources for spiritual transformation today come from authors of feminist poetry and literature, many of whom are black womanist poets, novelists, and writers. For an understanding of the term "womanist," see Alice Walker, *In Search of Our Mothers' Gardens: Womanist Prose* (New York: Harcourt Brace Jovanovich, 1983), and Katie Geneva Cannon, "The Emergence of Black Feminist Consciousness," in *Feminist Interpretation of the Bible,* ed. Letty M. Russell, pp. 30–40.

37. Frank Lentricchia explores this point brilliantly in his *Criticism and Social Change* (Chicago: University of Chicago Press, 1983).

38. Augustine, *On Christian Doctrine,* trans. D. W. Robertson, Jr. (Indianapolis, IN: Bobbs-Merrill, 1958), pp. 7–33.

39. Though I disagree with his constructive position, Mark C. Taylor's analysis of Word in *Erring* is an important interpretation; see especially, p. 7. See also Lacan, *Feminine Sexuality: Jacques Lacan and the Ecole Freudienne,* ed. Juliet Mitchell and Jacqueline Rose, trans. Jacqueline Rose (New York: Norton and Pantheon, 1985); and Burke, *The Rhetoric of Religion,* pp. 17–27. The point I want to make is that the Word became configured as a kind of primal signifier for patriarchal-monotheistic ordering in subjectivity, language, and politics.

40. There are numerous books on this subject, indeed, most books in feminist theory will touch on this topic in some manner. For a sampling see Cameron, *Feminism and Linguistic Theory;* Marks and Courtivron, eds., *New French Feminisms;* Moi, *Sexual/Textual Politics;* and Adrienne Rich, *On Lies, Secrets and Silence: Selected Prose 1966-78* (New York: Norton, 1979).

41. Morton, *The Journey Is Home,* pp. 40–61.

42. Kristeva, "About Chinese Women," p. 140.

43. What I am calling a monotheistic ordering—the securing of and by a primal referent "God" or "Man" by casting woman always as other and under—became, it seems to me, the hidden ordering of patriarchy in Christianity. While I have great respect for radical monotheism like H. Richard Neibuhr's, and I understand it to be a claim about God's transcendence, it still seems the case that if the logical-rhetoric-linguistic argument of monotheistic ordering as it has developed in many forms of Christianity is followed, then the "One" and the ones it guarantees tempts self-protection by way of denying and oppressing the many.

44. The critic and skeptic may wonder on what grounds I argue for this other Word, and my answer will rely on what the pragmatists called retroductive warrants. I want to argue for this other Word, first, by arguing for its semiotic possibility, or what Kristeva would call the *chora* as the precondition of all language; second, by arguing for its poetical possibility in women's experience; third, by arguing for its interpretive possibility in the Scriptures (Word as wisdom, as *dabar,* as creation); and, fourth, by arguing for its rhetorical importance given the present Christian situation and the need to challenge much of the

accommodation of Christianity to modernity by giving voice to those on the margins. In retroductive warrants, explanation and proof are closely related and the hypothesis which they support must illuminate and transform experience. For the use of retroductive warrants in theology, see Francis Schüssler Fiorenza, *Foundational Theology*, pp. 306–10.

45. This best describes the work of Julia Kristeva as compared to other French women writers such as Luce Irigaray and Helen Cixous. See Kristeva, *Revolution in Poetic Language*, trans. Leon S. Roudiez (New York: Columbia University Press, 1984), and idem, *Desire in Language: A Semiotic Approach to Literature and Art*, trans. Thomas Gora, Alice Jardine, and Leon S. Roudiez (New York: Columbia University Press, 1980).

46. See Luce Irigaray, *Speculum of the Other Woman*, trans. Gillian C. Gill (Ithaca, NY: Cornell University Press, 1985); idem, *Ce sexs qui n'en est pas un* (Paris: Editons de Minuit, 1977); and Helene Cixous, "The Laugh of the Medusa," in *New French Feminisms: An Anthology*, ed. Marks and Courtivron, pp. 245–64.

47. For interpretations of the discourses of the Virgin Mary, see Marina Warner, *Alone of All Her Sex: The Myth and the Cult of the Virgin Mary* (London: Wiedenfield, 1976), and Julia Kristeva, "Stabat Mater," in *Tales of Love*, trans. Leon S. Roudiez (New York: Columbia University Press, 1987), pp. 234–63. For an interpretation of the discourses of the cult of womanhood in the United States, see Sheila M. Rothman, *Woman's Proper Place: A History of Changing Ideals and Practices, 1870 to the Present* (New York: Basic Books, 1978).

48. Note that I use the phrase "intimately linked" only in terms of historical ordering. There is no "natural" or "metaphysical" reason that women and Word of creation and transformation, as the very precondition of subjectivity, language, and politics, have to be denied and repressed.

49. Though modernity leaves God-talk behind, it continues the basic monotheistic ordering in reference to "man" or full humanity as a code word for man. For a theological account of this, see Johannes Baptist Metz, *Theology of the World*, trans. William Glen-Doeple (New York: Seabury Press, 1969). An article in *Newsweek* on the environment makes much the same point: "who could have imagined man himself rendering the earth uninhabitable? We drew the wrong lesson from the Copernican revolution. In the Middle Ages, global warming—of several thousand degrees—was considered a very real threat, although mostly to sinners. The demonstration that the solar system was governed by natural laws undermined the belief that God might at any time smite it with fire. Since then, we have tended to assume the contrary: that the earth and its complex machinery would continue into the indefinite future as they have for the billions of years leading up to this moment. We forgot the one force capable of upsetting the balance that it took those billions of years to create. Ourselves" (July 11, 1988, p. 16).

50. Part of the difficulty in developing the theological possibility of the Word in relation to feminist discourses of emancipatory transformation is the need to incorporate a wide variety of linguistic sources within a theological formulation, to borrow, as our Burkean reversal suggests, from words about words to make the case for the Word. Thus we must expect the genre, as well as the substance,

of theology to change. I am indebted to Mary Gerhardt in a meeting of the Workgroup on Constructive Theology, June 1988 in Atlanta, Georgia, for pointing out the importance of genre to theology.

51. In *Honey-Mad Women,* Yaeger suggests a new mythology of women's writing, and to see this as part of the past tradition of women writing, as well as in the present and promised for the future, takes issues with Cixous and Irigaray, for celebrating only the present and the future prospects of women's speech. The point is to celebrate this way of speaking, to see it as the way women have always "played" in and with words and the way such speech has always been divine speaking, or as Yeager says, "French feminists' texts are not just attempts to challenge the patriarchal tradition; they want to devise a mode of feminine 'Sondersprache,' to discover a tradition that will allow us to read feminine speech as divine speech, as mystified writing. But while I find the French feminists' emphasis on a redeemed orality breathtaking, I want to insist that Wittig, Cixous, Irigaray, and the other writers quoted here *do not go far enough* in defining this orality. *'Ecriture féminine'* names the writing of the future—but to claim it as our own we must be permitted to see its features in the writing of the past" (p. 16).

52. A theological semiotics and pragmatics is necessary if one takes seriously discourse as a theological and religious activity and accepts that language and discourse do not just reflect the world, but indeed constitute reality and transform it.

53. For a general introduction to semiotics, see Umberto Eco, *Semiotics and the Philosophy of Language* (Bloomington: Indiana University Press, 1984), and *Soviet Semiotics: An Anthology,* ed. and trans. Daniel P. Lucid (Baltimore: John Hopkins University Press, 1977).

54. Peirce, *Collected Papers* 5:180–205.

55. The notion of sign as perfectly open is not to deny the historicality of any particular sign, indeed the reliance on pragmatism and rhetoric would prohibit such a denial. It is, rather, to entitle the reality of multiplicity and otherness in the signification of the God term, which, in turn, blesses and promotes multiplicity and otherness in language and discourse.

56. Kristeva, *Revolution in Poetic Language,* pp. 21–106.

57. Jürgen Moltmann, in *Theology of Hope: On the Ground and the Implications of a Christian Eschatology* (San Francisco: Harper & Row, 1967), interpreted this notion of God's name as "I will be who I will be" as a God before us, in the future. Actually, Moltmann seems to offer two interpretations: one in which "I will be" is a kind of neoorthodox unconnectedness cast into the future; the second, an intertwining of "overfilling" possibilities and new transformations in a kind of aesthetic interpretation of God's activity. See Rebecca S. Chopp, *The Praxis of Suffering: An Interpretation of Liberation and Political Theologies* (Maryknoll, NY: Orbis, 1986), pp. 100–117, and Christopher Morse, *The Logic of Promise in Moltmann's Theology* (Philadelphia: Fortress Press, 1975).

58. Burke, *The Rhetoric of Religion,* pp. 14–15.

59. Ibid., p. 40.

60. Ibid., p. 15.

61. Word may be said to transcend words but it is not, at least in this theology of the Word, wholly other to words. See Burke's second analogy: "Words are to the nonverbal things they name as Spirit is to Matter" (pp. 16–17).

62. Heilbrun, *Writing a Woman's Life*, p. 128.

63. Jürgen Moltmann, *The Trinity and the Kingdom: The Doctrine of God* (San Francisco: Harper & Row, 1981).

64. See Chopp, *The Praxis of Suffering*, pp. 24–25.

65. Marge Piercy, "For Strong Women," in *The Moon Is Always Female*, pp. 56–57.

66. Samuel Weber, *Institution and Interpretation*, Theory and History of Literature, vol. 31 (Minneapolis: University of Minnesota Press, 1987), p. 12; and Robert S. Corrington, *The Community of Interpreters: On the Hermeneutics of Nature and the Bible in the American Philosophical Tradition*, Studies in American Biblical Hermeneutics 3 (Macon, GA: Mercer University Press, 1987).

67. Peirce, *Collected Papers* 5:416.

68. Burke, *The Rhetoric of Religion*, p. 8.

69. For the notion of anticipatory freedom, see Chopp, *The Praxis of Suffering*, pp. 125–26; for this notion in relation to semiotics and pragmatism, see Karl-Otto Apel, *Charles S. Peirce: From Pragmatism to Pragmaticism*, trans. John M. Krois (Amherst: University of Massachusetts Press, 1981), pp. 99–103.

70. Though we might hope to retrieve the term "conversion" for transformation, in our present situation transformation suggests forming anew, while conversion, at least in current discourse, suggests a change from one set of details to another.

71. As in Peirce, pragmatism is related to semiotics, or the logic of meaning is related to how signs operate. See H. S. Thayer, *Meaning and Action: A Critical History of Pragmatism* (Indianapolis, IN: Hackett, 1968, 1981), pp. 86–101.

72. Meaning, in this sense, has to do with what illuminates, guides, and transforms human activity. See John Dewey, *Reconstruction in Philosophy* (New York: New American Library of World Literature, 1950), p. 128; idem, *Experience and Nature*, rev. ed. (New York: Norton, 1929), p. 188; and Francis Schüssler Fiorenza, *Foundational Theology*, pp. 307–8.

73. Peirce, *Collected Papers* 5:180–205. Mary Jacobus advocates abduction as a strategy of leading away meaning in feminist theory, though without any identifiable reference to Peirce. Jacobus's use of the term signals for me serious problems in that abduction has come to mean kidnapping, and is a term connected to violence in our society. See Mary Jacobus, *Reading Woman: Essays in Feminist Criticism* (New York: Columbia University Press, 1986). The other term Peirce used is *retroduction*, but that term is also problematic since it carries connotations of reduction. I have chosen to keep the term I sense Peirce preferred, though with qualified hesitation.

74. Peirce, *Collected Papers* 5:180–205.

75. Ibid., 5:172.

76. Ibid., 5:151–74.

77. John Dewey, *Art as Experience* (New York: Minton, Blach, 1931).

78. Play is a term used widely in contemporary philosophy, often with quite

different meanings. Hans Georg Gadamer uses "play" to speak of a game with rules, but rules so well-known that the game takes over; Derrida uses "play" more in the sense of free play. Following Patricia Yaeger, I use "play" in the sense of the creation of new possibilities (*Honey-Mad Women*, pp. 207–38).

79. Yaeger, *Honey-Mad Women*, p. 231.

80. Weedon, *Feminist Practice and Poststructuralist Theory*, pp. 80–85. For theological interpretations of demythologizing humanism, see Tracy, *Plurality and Ambiguity*, pp. 55–59, and Taylor, *Erring*, pp. 34–73. For a feminist account, see Moi, *Sexual/Textual Politics*, pp. 21–88. For a postmodern anthropology, see Stephen A. Tyler, *The Unspeakable: Discourse, Dialogue, and Rhetoric in the Postmodern World* (Madison: University of Wisconsin Press, 1987).

81. Terry Eagleton, in *Against the Grain: Essays 1975–1985* (London: Verso, 1986), puts this quite eloquently: "Rhetoric, in other words, precedes logic: grasping propositions is only possible by participating in specific forms of social life" (p. 169). In another work he makes the point this way: "Rhetoric, which was the received form of critical analysis all the way from ancient society to the eighteenth century, examined the way discourses are constructed in order to achieve certain effects. It was not worried about whether its objects of enquiry were speaking or writing, poetry or philosophy, fiction or historiography: its horizon was nothing less than the field of discursive practices in society as a whole, and its particular interest lay in grasping such practices as forms of power and performance. This is not to say that it ignored the truth-value of the discourses in question, since this could often be crucially relevant to the kinds of effect they produced in their readers and listeners. Rhetoric in its major phase was neither a 'humanism', concerned in some intuitive way with people's experience of language, nor a 'formalism' preoccupied simply with analyzing linguistic devices. It looked at such devices in terms of concrete-performance—they were means of pleading, persuading, inciting and so on—and at people's responses to discourse in terms of linguistic structures and the material situation in which they functioned" (*Literary Theory*, pp. 205–6).

82. Discourses that come close to being pure discourses of fundamental attitudes could be called epidectic discourses. Epidectic is one of three oratorical genres. *Epidectic* has to do with an audience enjoying, *deliberative* with an audience speculating, and *forensic* with an audience judging. Epidectic discourses, in the rhetoric of this text, could be considered discourses of fundamental attitudes concerning the beautiful. See Aristotle, *Rhetoric* I. 3. 1358b. 2–7; for a contemporary account, see Ch. Perelman and L. Olbrechts-Tyteca, *The New Rhetoric: A Treatise on Argumentation*, trans. John Wilkinson and Purcell Weaver (Notre Dame: University of Notre Dame Press, 1969).

Chapter 2: The Power of Freedom: Proclamation and Scripture

Epigraph: Ernst Bloch, *Atheism in Christianity: The Religion of the Exodus and the Kingdom*, trans. J. T. Swann (New York: Herder and Herder, 1972), p. 26.

1. For examples of feminist biblical hermeneutics, see Elisabeth Schüssler Fiorenza, *In Memory of Her;* Phyllis Trible, *God and the Rhetoric of Sexuality* (Philadelphia: Fortress Press, 1978); idem, *Texts of Terror* (Philadelphia: Fortress Press,

1984); and Katherine Doob Sakenfeld, *Faithfulness in Action: Loyalty in Biblical Perspective* (Philadelphia: Fortress Press, 1985). For discussions on the question, see the essays collected in *Feminist Interpretation of the Bible,* ed. Letty M. Russell.

2. The best general discussion of the use of Scripture in modern theology remains David Kelsey's *The Uses of Scripture in Recent Theology* (Philadelphia: Fortress Press, 1975).

3. For a good account of the dialogical relation between Scripture and experience, see Paul Ricoeur, "Naming God," trans. David Pellauer, *Union Seminary Quarterly Review* 34 (Summer 1979): 215–27.

4. Of course, we can only understand the *status* of the Scriptures as proclamations, that is, as forms of Christian discourse, for their substance must be queried as to the possibility, including the historical reality, of emancipatory transformation (thus constituting a hermeneutics of marginality). I am suggesting that feminist theology consider the Scriptures as the prototypical documents of discursive practices of the Christian community, i.e., how Christians, in the context of community, constituted and expressed their Christian witness.

5. There are, of course, numerous ways to arrive at the theological judgment about what constitutes credible claims of freedom. For two examples focused on Christological arguments, see Schubert Ogden, *The Point of Christology* (New York: Harper & Row, 1982), and Ernst Käsemann, *Jesus Means Freedom* (Philadelphia: Fortress Press, 1969). Elisabeth Schüssler Fiorenza in *In Memory of Her* focuses her judgment on community witness, both present and past.

6. Elisabeth Schüssler Fiorenza has suggested "a feminist critical hermeneutics of suspicion places a warning label on all biblical texts: *Caution! Could be dangerous to your health and survival*" ("The Will to Choose or to Reject: Continuing Our Critical Work," in *Feminist Interpretation of the Bible,* p. 130).

7. For one example of how the Scriptures are still used in the abuse of women and how they can be used in the self-affirmation of women, see Susan Brooks Thistlethwaite, "Every Two Minutes: Battered Women and Feminist Interpretation," in *Feminist Interpretation of the Bible,* pp. 96–107.

8. Elisabeth Schüssler Fiorenza, *In Memory of Her,* especially pp. 26–36, and idem, *Bread Not Stone,* pp. 9–11. As compared to Elisabeth Schüssler Fiorenza's use of Scripture as prototype, I prefer to speak of the Scriptures as prototypes. The consistent use of the plural indicates the multiplicity of discourses within the Bible.

9. Elisabeth Schüssler Fiorenza, *Bread Not Stone,* pp. xvi–xvii.

10. Ibid., xvii. In note 21 on p. 153, Elisabeth Schüssler Fiorenza clarifies what she means by this notion of revelation in the community: "My position is often misunderstood as postulating a period of equality in the earliest beginnings of the church, which very soon was superseded by the patriarchal form of church. My point, however, is not only that the 'discipleship' of equals preceded the 'patriarchalization' of church but also that it was repressed rather than replaced. Although the discipleship community of equals or women-church was submerged and often oppressed by ecclesiastical patriarchy, it has never ceased to exist. Rather than conceptualize church history as a history of decline (or progress, dependent on the point of view) I conceptualize it as a history of strug-

gle. Insofar as the Bible is the model for both women-church *and* patriarchal church, it is also the paradigm of this struggle." I disagree somewhat with E. Schüssler Fiorenza about the adequacy of the conceptuality of this history of struggle, preferring to give warrants for the notion of revelation in the community in relation to the present material norm of credible claims of freedom which can take account of historical testimony. For yet a third option of revelation, community, and Scripture, see Ronald F. Thiemann, *Revelation and Theology: The Gospel as Narrated Promise* (Notre Dame, IN: University of Notre Dame Press, 1985).

11. Elisabeth Schüssler Fiorenza, *Bread Not Stone*, p. xvii.

12. Ibid., pp. 15–22.

13. I am indebted to Katharine Doob Sakenfeld's article, "Feminist Uses of Biblical Materials," in *Feminist Interpretation of the Bible*, pp. 55–64, for identifying and classifying the various ways feminists have used the Bible.

14. Biblical symbols, in the words of Langdon Gilkey, "challenge the way we concretely are, they call for a new way of being, a new attitude to ourselves and to others, for forms of actual relations in community and a new kind of action in the world" (*Reaping the Whirlwind: A Christian Interpretation of History* [New York: Seabury, 1976], p. 138).

15. For an excellent account of how Scripture has functioned throughout much of Christian theology and the need to abandon any remnants of the scriptural principle and the house of authority in the present context, see Edward Farley, *Ecclesial Reflection: An Anatomy of Theological Method* (Philadelphia: Fortress Press, 1982), esp. pp. 47–82.

16. These six questions are asked to the text, but are themselves taken from readings of the text. They are influenced, as well, by Kenneth Burke's notion of dramatism and its five key terms: act, scene, agent, agency, and purpose, in *A Grammar of Motives*. For an interpretation of Burke's dramatology see William H. Rueckert, *Kenneth Burke and the Drama of Human Relations*, 2nd ed. (Berkeley and Los Angeles: University of California Press, 1963, 1982).

17. For the notion of dialogue when reading a "classic," see David Tracy, *The Analogical Imagination: Christian Theology and the Culture of Pluralism* (New York: Crossroad, 1981), pp. 99–124.

18. For the role of appropriation in interpretation, see Hans-Georg Gadamer, *Truth and Method*, trans. ed. Garrett Barden and John Cumming, (New York: Seabury, 1975), pp. 275–305. For discussion of appropriation in Gadamer's hermeneutics, see David Couzens Hoy, *The Critical Circle: Literature, History and Hermeneutics* (Berkeley and Los Angeles: University of California Press, 1978), pp. 51–54, and Richard J. Bernstein, *Beyond Objectivism and Relativism: Science, Hermeneutics, and Praxis* (Philadelphia: University of Pennsylvania Press, 1983), pp. 144–50.

19. For a related criticism of modernity through its ordering of time, see Metz, *Faith In History and Society*, pp. 165–74, and Walter Benjamin, *Illuminations*, ed. Hannah Arendt, trans. Harry Zohn (New York: Schocken, 1969), pp. 253–64.

20. Friedrich Schleiermacher, *Christmas Eve: Dialogues on the Incarnation*, trans. Terrence N. Tice (Richmond, VA: John Knox Press, 1967).

21. Karl Barth, *The Epistle to the Romans*, trans. Edwyn C. Hoskyns (London: Oxford University Press, 1933).

22. Paul Tillich, *Systematic Theology* 3:369–72.

23. See, for instance, Karl Rahner, *Christian Foundations*. Rahner's brillance at working within the modern formulation of time and existential existence, while retrieving traditional Christian doctrines, is illustrated in many places, but certainly one of the most moving is his often overlooked *On the Theology of Death*, trans. C. H. Henkey (New York: Seabury Press, 1961).

24. See, for instance, John Locke, *Two Treatises of Government*, ed. Peter Laslett (London: Cambridge University Press, 1960).

25. Joseph Fitzmyer, *The Gospel According to Luke I–IX*, Anchor Bible 28 (Garden City, NY: Doubleday, 1981), p. 227, and Hans Conzelmann, *The Theology of St. Luke* (New York: Harper, 1960).

26. In this sense, the Spirit is relational, not psychological. The Spirit, as moving out from God and Christ in a trinitarian perspective, likewise moves out from Christian community and its witness to the world. See Moltmann, *The Trinity and the Kingdom*, pp. 122–29.

27. Gutiérrez, *Theology of Liberation*, p. 108, and idem, "Theology and Spirituality in a Latin American Context" *Harvard Divinity Bulletin* 14 (June–August 1984): 4.

28. Luke 6:20–26. Luke's "option for the poor and oppressed" is commented on in many studies; see, for example, Eduard Schweizer, *The Good News According to Luke*, trans. David E. Green (Atlanta: John Knox Press, 1984), p. 119. For an excellent study on the poor in Luke, see Luke T. Johnson, *Sharing Possessions: Mandate and Symbol of Faith* (Philadelphia: Fortress Press, 1981).

29. Eduard Schweizer, *Luke: A Challenge to Present Theology* (Atlanta: John Knox Press, 1982), p. 52. I do not want to indicate that Luke himself was particularly interested in the emancipation of women, since women appear in Luke's Gospel in quite traditional ways. I am indebted to Kathleen Waller for discussion on this point.

30. Luke 21:1–4; Luke 14:12–24; Luke 10:38–42.

31. The genealogical account follows Jesus' baptism, and is unique in tracing Jesus' heritage back to God; see M. D. Johnson, *The Purpose of the Biblical Genealogies with Special Reference to the Setting of the Genealogies of Jesus*, Studiorum Novi Testamenti Societas, Monograph Series 8 (Cambridge: University Press, 1969), p. 237. In *The Good News According to Luke*, Schweizer comments about Luke's tracing of Jesus' genealogy all the way back to God: "All that matters to him [Luke], is the line that runs from God, the father of Adam and thus of all humanity (Acts 17:28–29), to Jesus, suggesting the solidarity of Jesus with all humankind" (p. 80).

32. Fitzmyer, *The Gospel According to Luke*, pp. 18–22, 179–92. There is no consensus among Lucan scholars about whether two or three phases of salvation history should be identified in Luke. Conzelmann, in *Theology*, argues for

three, while W. G. Kummel, in "Current Theology Accusations against Luke" *Andover Newton Quarterly* 16 (1975): 131–45, argues for two. But the whole notion of the adequacy of salvation history as an interpretive framework of Luke is also being questioned in Lucan scholarship. For instance, Jacob Jervell has argued that, in Luke, the church is not a new era, a new Israel, in effect, in salvation history, arguing that it is important for Luke to show that the Jewish Christian church is a part of Israel. See Jacob Jervell, *Luke and the People of God: A New Look at Luke-Acts* (Minneapolis, MN: Augsburg, 1972). Whether or not Jervell is correct (and his argument seems very persuasive), it can still be said that the text uses and transforms the jubilee images to proclaim emancipatory transformation, though perhaps not in a "new," but in a different, era of historical realization.

33. Fitzmyer, *The Gospel According to Luke,* p. 21.

34. Schweizer, *Luke,* especially pp. 13–26.

35. It is important to call attention again to Jervell's argument that for Luke the church is not the new Israel but, in a sense, the real Israel, or in Jervell's words, "Luke is rather concerned to show that when the gospel was preached, the one people of God, of the one and only Israel, continues among those obedient Jews who believe in Jesus. The promises given to Israel are being fulfilled among the Jewish Christians" (*Luke and the People of God,* p. 15). But in relation to what this means about the nature of testimony, it still seems as if the case can be made that testimony must be given to the reordering of all relations, a reordering that now spreads throughout gentile as well as Jewish communities. See especially, "The Divided People of God," in *Luke and the People of God,* pp. 41–74.

36. I am indebted to the provocative reading of the jubilee images by Sharon H. Ringe, in *Jesus, Liberation, and the Biblical Jubilee: Images for Ethics and Christology* (Philadelphia: Fortress Press, 1985).

37. Fitzmyer, *The Gospel According to Luke,* p. 149.

38. It is important to note that Jesus, by anticipating their response and having already invoked the divine origin of his message, functionally places both himself and his hearers on trial.

39. I am indebted to Paul Ricoeur's "The Hermeneutics of Testimony," in *Essays on Biblical Interpretation,* ed. Lewis S. Mudge (Philadelphia: Fortress Press, 1980), pp. 119–54 for an interpretive framework for this section. By prophetic concept of testimony Ricoeur means testimony as oriented toward proclamation which proceeds from a "an absolute initiative as to its origin and its content" (p. 131).

40. Ibid.

41. Ibid., p. 133.

42. Ibid., pp. 144–45.

43. Ibid., pp. 151–52.

44. Fitzmyer's explanation of this story is fairly standard: "The Lucan story, transposed to this point in the gospel, has a definite programmatic character. Jesus's teaching is a fulfillment of OT Scripture—this is his kerygmatic announcement (the Lucan substitute for the omitted proclamation of Mark 1:

14b–15). But that same teaching will meet with success and—even more so—with rejection. Luke has deliberately put this story at the beginning of the public ministry to encapsulate the entire ministry of Jesus and the reaction to it. The fulfillment-story stresses the success of his teaching under the guidance of the Spirit, but the rejection story symbolizes the opposition that his ministry will evoke among his own. The rejection of him by the people of his hometown is a miniature of the rejection by the people of his own *patris* in the larger sense" (p. 529).

45. Recall the traditional axiom: "Men are usually right in what they affirm, wrong in what they deny"; a truth which this text seems to reverse.

46. Fitzmyer, *The Gospel According to Luke*, p. 529.

47. In referring to the prophetic image, I am speaking of the use of material from what biblical scholars call the prophetic tradition as compared to the priestly tradition. It is often the case that theologians ascribe liberationist sayings to the prophetic tradition while treating the priestly tradition with scorn. This passage, interestingly, reverses the priority, where liberation themes come from priestly tradition. I am indebted to my colleague John Hayes for this insight.

48. The biblical scholars' explanation of conflation, displaces the shift in mood through the bringing together of two different stories. The reader, who is not immediately concerned with the sources of this text, is struck by the difference in mood. In the space of a few brief phrases, the reader is moved from the soaring heights of fulfillment, exaltation, promise, and newness, to the depths of rejection, violence, and escape.

49. The relationship between theology and historical-critical scholarship of the Bible is, by now, filled with tension and at an impasse. Theologians who claim that the Bible discloses the real to us, or that the Bible names our reality, have more in common with each other than with Biblical scholars, for whom the Bible becomes a historical book to be discovered, explored, and explained. This is not to be critical of the task of biblical scholars or that of theologians, but simply to note that this ordering too is a symbolic construct (after all, the great Reformation theologian Luther was a professor of Bible) and may change again.

50. Origen, for instance, suggests that there are three levels of Scripture, literal, moral, and spiritual (see *On First Principles* 4.2.4), while Augustine discusses the ambiguity of Scripture in relation to literal and figurative signs, urging the rule of *caritas* for interpretation (*On Christian Doctrine*, 3.10.16). As D. W. Robertson points out in his introduction to *On Christian Doctrine* Augustine regarded the diversity of meanings in the Scriptures, yielded through allegorical interpretation, as a virtue not a shortcoming (p. xi).

51. Barth, Tillich, and Bultmann all bring some type of Christological principle to bear on the authority and interpretation of Scripture. For Barth, Scripture witnesses to the event of Jesus Christ; for Tillich, Scripture is authoritative as it provides the picture of Jesus Christ, while for Bultmann Scripture has authority through the mediation of the Christ event.

52. See Ringe, *Jesus, Liberation and the Biblical Jubilee.*

53. Proclamation, at least in the intent of this book, includes preaching as an

exercise of public speaking in a worship service, but is not confined to it. Indeed, the substance and task of proclamation now has to do with the Good News for the world, not the existential, moral, or institutional maintenance of the church.

54. The best theological account of this concupiscence remains that of Tillich in *Systematic Theology* 1:51–55.

55. By *habits* I mean patterns of behavior that follow laws and rules. See Peirce, *Collected Papers* 5:538 and Richard Bernstein, *Praxis and Action: Contemporary Philosophies of Human Activity* (Philadelphia: University of Pennsylvania Press, 1971), pp. 184–87.

Chapter 3: The Community of Emancipatory Transformation

Epigraph: Kristeva, *Desire in Language*, p. 25.

1. John Hope Franklin, *From Slavery to Freedom: A History of Negro Americans*, 3rd ed. (New York: Vintage, 1969); Gayraud Wilmore, *Black Religion and Black Radicalism*, 2nd ed. (Maryknoll, NY: Orbis, 1983); Albert J. Raboteau, *Slave Religion: The ''Invisible Institution'' in the Antebellum South* (New York: Oxford University Press, 1978); James Cone, *The Spirituals and the Blues* (New York: Seabury Press, 1972). I am also indebted to conversations with Robert Franklin, Peter Paris, and Noel Erskine.

2. Gutiérrez, *The Theology of Liberation;* Enrique D. Dussel, *A History of the Church in Latin America: Colonialism to Liberation (1492–1979)*, trans. Alan Neely (Grand Rapids, MI: Eerdmans, 1981); Penny Lernoux, *The Cry of the People: The Struggle for Human Rights in Latin America—The Catholic Church in Conflict with U.S. Policy* (New York: Penguin, 1980); *The Challenge of Basic Christian Communities: Papers from the International Ecumenical Congress of Theology*, ed. Sergio Torres and John Eagleson (Maryknoll, NY: Orbis, 1981); and Jon Sobrino, *The True Church and the Poor*, trans. Matthew J. O'Connell (Maryknoll, NY: Orbis, 1984).

3. Metz, *The Emergent Church*, pp. 1–16.

4. I am indebted to Kris Culp for her work on women-church in her thesis, ''The Church of Women and Redemptive Community: A Proposal for a North American Post-Patriarchal Ecclesiology with Implications for a Method of Feminist Theology,'' (in progress) at The Divinity School, University of Chicago.

5. For an excellent account of the feminist movement in American churches, see Anne E. Carr, *Transforming Grace: Christian Tradition and Women's Experience* (San Francisco: Harper & Row, 1988).

6. Ibid., p. 9–10; see also the introduction to *Womanspirit Rising: A Feminist Reader in Religion*, ed. Christ and Plaskow, pp. 9–11.

7. The movement from being a corrective in the church (with emphasis placed on things such as women's ordination) to a transformation of the church, a type of ''new'' reformation, seems especially clear in recent works by Rosemary Radford Ruether, such as *Women-Church: Theology and Practice of Feminist Liturgical Communities* (San Francisco: Harper & Row, 1985) and *Sexism and God-Talk;* and in Elisabeth Schüssler Fiorenza's *In Memory of Her*, pp. 343–51, and *Bread Not Stone*, pp. 1–22. See also Beverly Wildung Harrison, *Making the Connections: Essays in Feminist Social Ethics*, ed. Carol S. Robb (Boston: Beacon Press, 1985), pp. 191–263.

8. Ruether, *Women-Church*, p. 72.

9. Ibid., p. 5. Note that this is no easy realization for Ruether: "We do not form new communities lightly, but only because the crisis has grown so acute and the efforts to effect change so unpromising that we often cannot even continue to communicate within these traditional church institutions unless we have an alternative community of reference that nurtures and supports our being."

10. Elisabeth Schüssler Fiorenza states: "*Ekklēsia*—the term for church in the New Testament—is not so much a religious as a civil-political concept. It means the actual assembly of free citizens gathering for deciding their own spiritual-political affairs. Since women in a patriarchal church cannot decide their own theological-religious affairs and that of their own people—women—the *ekklēsia* of women is as much a future hope as it is a reality today. Yet we have begun to gather as the *ekklēsia* of women, as the people of God, to claim our religious powers, to participate fully in the decision-making process of church, and to nurture each other as women Christians" (*In Memory of Her*, p. 344).

11. Ibid.

12. I am in agreement with Hodgson's interpretation of women-church as "*within* and *on the edges* of the institution, refusing to leave it as sectarian or schismatic groups but also refusing to fit into it on its own terms, working to transform it without being stifled or controlled by it. In this respect women-church follows a traditional Catholic pattern of remaining within the *ecclesia catholica* rather than the Protestant sectarian pattern of starting a new church. Women-church is an 'institution' only in a loose sense; it has more the character of a grass-roots movement in which local groups form spontaneously and for which there is only a skeletal organization but an active communications network" (*Revisioning the Church*, pp. 86–87). But women-church promises to be much more than this. It promises, I am suggesting, to be a new reformation of the church. For the notion of new reformation, see Metz, *The Emergent Church*, pp. 48–66, where he argues that the movement of basic Christian communities leads to a new reformation.

13. Ruether says it most poignantly: "Women in contemporary churches are suffering from linguistic deprivation and eucharistic famine. They can no longer nurture their souls in alienating words that ignore or systematically deny their existence. They are starved for the words of life, for symbolic forms that fully and wholeheartedly affirm their personhood and speak truth about the evils of sexism and the possibilities of a future beyond patriarchy" (*Women-Church*, pp. 4–5).

14. See, for instance, Robert N. Bellah et al., *Habits of the Heart: Individualism and Commitment in American Life* (San Francisco: Harper & Row, 1985), pp. 219–49, 275–96.

15. See, for instance, Richard B. Wilke, *And Are We Yet Alive: The Future of the United Methodist Church* (Nashville: Abingdon Press, 1986).

16. Moltmann, "Exodus Church: Observations on the Eschatological Understanding of Christianity in Modern Society," *Theology of Hope*, pp. 304–38; see also idem, *The Passion for Life: A Messianic Lifestyle*, trans. M. Douglas Meeks (Philadelphia: Fortress Press, 1978).

17. Moltmann, *Theology of Hope*, pp. 307–11.

18. Ibid., pp. 311–24.

19. Moltmann's analysis of the implications of the cult of individualism for theology is excellent, and deserves to be quoted at length: "In harmony with this romanticist metaphysic of subjecthood and this mental attitude of constant metaphysical reflection there then appears also the theology which takes the cult of the absolute that has become of no significance in our social relationships and cultivates it as the transcendent background of modern existence. This is the theology which presents itself as 'doctrine of the faith' and finds the place of faith in the transcendental subjectivity of man. It is a theology of existence, for which 'existence' is the relation of man to himself as this emerges in the 'total reflection of man on himself.' . . . The modern metaphysic of subjecthood with its consequences in the secularization of the world must then be represented as a consequence of Christian faith, and Christian faith must be represented as the truth behind this metaphysic of subjecthood. . . . In this theology, Christian faith is transcendent as compared with everything meaningful that can be socially communicated. It is not provable—but its unprovability, so it is said, is its very strength—and consequently it is also irrefutable. Unbelief alone, as being the contrary decision, is its enemy. As constant reflection it cannot be given institutional form, but is itself transcendence as compared with social institutions. It has primarily to do with 'self-understanding' of the human subject in the technical world. It sees 'God' not as a God of the world or of history or of society, but rather as the unconditioned in the conditional, the beyond in the things of this world, the transcendent in the present" (*Theology of Hope*, pp. 313–14).

20. Ibid., p. 312; see also Brown, *Society as Text*, pp. 35–36.

21. For a critique of Moltmann's methodological dialectics of contradiction and how it fails to carry through his own, often excellent, interpretive dialectics of identification, see Chopp, *The Praxis of Suffering*, pp. 100–117.

22. Moltmann, *Theology of Hope*, p. 320.

23. The theologies of Friedrich Schleiermacher and Karl Barth have often, even usually, been seen as completely opposed to one another. For new interpretations of how much these theologians had in common, see *Barth and Schleiermacher: Beyond the Impasse*, ed. James O. Duke and Robert F. Streetman (Philadelphia: Fortress Press, 1988).

24. Friedrich Schleiermacher, *The Christian Faith*, ed. H. R. MacKintosh and J. S. Stewart (Edinburgh: T. & T. Clark, and Philadelphia: Fortress Press, 1928, 1976), 87.1 (pp. 358–61), see also the section on the church, 115–126 (pp. 532–85).

25. Ibid., 123 (p. 569).

26. Karl Barth, *Evangelical Theology: An Introduction*, trans. Grover Foley (Grand Rapids, MI: Eerdmans, 1963), p. 38.

27. I am using Schleiermacher and Barth to reconstruct the notion of church as community. In a sense I am using them to develop a logic of Christian community, an ecclesiology, beginning with how community is grounded in the Word (now as perfectly open sign), its corporate nature, and how this constitutes its piety. In using Schleiermacher and Barth, I also want to underscore the possibility of using modern theology reconstructively and transformatively. It is

not the case that feminists must renounce patriarchal theologies; rather, feminists must criticize and transform them into proclamations of emancipatory transformation.

28. Hodgson suggests that the early church had to develop such a poetics, an elaboration of images and metaphors, in relation to *ecclesia:* "The community of believers in Jesus Christ did not attempt to form a cultic title from the name Jesus, and only later did they come to be known as Christians. . . . Rather, as we have seen, the preferred term of self-designation was '*ecclesia,*' taken over with its Greek, Septuagint, and Hellenistic Jewish connotations but functioning as a formal term that required theological elaboration. This elaboration was provided by a profusion of metaphors and images from ordinary language and everyday experience. The metaphorical process that began with the parables and sayings of Jesus continued to characterize the way that believers thought and talked about God, redemption, the Messiah, and themselves; in a profound sense, Christianity was and remains a language-event" (*Revisioning the Church,* p. 28). See also Paul Minear, *Images of the Church in the New Testament* (Philadelphia: Westminister Press, 1960).

29. Note, for instance, Barth's brilliant poetics of the church in his comparison of the church of Esau and the church of Isaac, in *The Epistle to the Romans,* pp. 330–61.

30. Elisabeth Schüssler Fiorenza links communion, community, and the communicative praxis (or rhetoric) of the church in this manner: "In the Greek Old Testament *ekklēsia* means the 'assembly of the people of Israel before God.' In the New Testament *ekklēsia* comes through the agency of the Spirit to visible, tangible expression in and through the gathering of God's people around the table, eating together a meal, breaking the bread, and sharing the cup in memory of Christ's passion and resurrection. *Christian* spirituality means eating together, sharing together, drinking together, talking with each other, receiving each other, experiencing God's presence through each other, and, in doing so, proclaiming the gospel as God's alternative vision for everyone, especially for those who are poor, outcast, and battered" (*In Memory of Her,* p. 345). See also Johannes B. Metz, "Bread of Survival: The Lord's Supper of Christians as Anticipatory Sign of an Anthropological Revolution," in *The Emergent Church,* pp. 34–47.

31. Walter Ong, *The Presence of the Word: Some Prolegomena for Cultural and Religious History* (Minneapolis: University of Minnesota Press, 1967); see also idem, *Orality and Literacy: The Technologizing of the Word* (New York: Methuen, 1986) and *Interfaces of the Word: Studies in the Evolution of Consciousness and Culture* (Ithaca, NY: Cornell University Press, 1977).

32. It is at this point that we can reintroduce the notion of a sermon in the context of liturgy as one of the aesthetic practices of the community. The sermon thus arises out of the community and is always located as part of the liturgy and not, as so often is the case in Protestantism, the "main event" with the liturgy as time-filler. See David Buttrick, *Homiletic: Moves and Structures* (Philadelphia: Fortress Press, 1987).

33. Dallymar, *Language and Politics,* pp. 178–79.

34. Especially in poetic language, images of the church must be multiple and

diverse. Minear, for instance, in *The Images of the Church in the New Testament* identifies ninety-six different images used in the New Testament.

35. For a contemporary work relating rhetoric and praxis, see Calvin O. Schrag, *Communicative Praxis and the Space of Subjectivity* (Bloomington: Indiana University Press, 1986).

36. I am calling for a communal dialogue with the Scriptures and am following the model of interpreting religious texts developed by Tracy in *The Analogical Imagination,* especially pp. 154–219.

37. Schrag, *Communicative Praxis and the Space of Subjectivity* pp. 179–96.

38. See Ch. Perelman and L. Olbrechts-Tyteca, *The New Rhetoric,* p. 1; see also Richard Rorty, *Philosophy and the Mirror of Nature* (Princeton, NJ: Princeton University Press, 1979).

39. For interpretations of ideology critique, see Raymond Geuss, *The Idea of a Critical Theory: Habermas and the Frankfurt School* (Cambridge: Cambridge University Press, 1981); David Held, *Introduction to Critical Theory: Horkheimer to Habermas* (Berkeley and Los Angeles: University of California Press, 1980); and Paul Connerton, *The Tragedy of Enlightenment: An Essay on the Frankfurt School* (Cambridge: Cambridge University Press, 1980).

40. Richard J. Bernstein, *Beyond Objectivism and Relativism: Science, Hermeneutics, and Praxis,* pp. 51–108.

41. Eagleton, *Against the Grain,* p. 169.

42. I am indebted to Susan Shapiro for not only introducing me to the study of rhetoric but also for her excellent analysis of rhetoric, ideology critique, and the modern world in a paper entitled, "Rhetoric as Ideology Critique: The Gadamer-Habermas Debate Reinvented," presented in the Rhetoric and Religious Discourse Section, American Academy of Religion, Annaheim, California, 1985.

43. An interesting possibility for one way of developing the deliberative nature of a community of emancipatory transformation is by the use of Jurgen Habermas's universal pragmatics to deliberate within the ongoing conversation. For an illustration of such a development, see Jens Glebe-Moller, *A Political Dogmatic,* trans. Thor Hall (Philadelphia: Fortress Press, 1982). Such a possibility would be developed within the life of the community and not as a universal quasi-transcendental basis of the community.

44. I am indebted to Richard J. Bernstein's reading of Gadamer at this point; see his "From Hermeneutics to Praxis," in *Philosophical Profiles: Essays in a Pragmatic Mode* (Philadelphia: University of Pennsylvania Press, 1986), pp. 94–114.

45. Metz, *The Emergent Church,* pp. 60–62.

46. Wayne Booth, *Critical Understanding: The Powers and Limits of Pluralism* (Chicago: University of Chicago Press, 1979), pp. 220–32.

47. Ibid. Booth links justice and vitality with the need for articulated critical understandings. See also Tracy, *Analogical Imagination,* pp. 121–23. I am, of course, using hermeneutical and rhetorical criteria to identify the virtues necessary for community discussion. For the relationship between hermeneutics and community see Bernstein, *Beyond Objectivism and Relativism,* pp. 223–31. Booth himself appeals to rhetorical criteria; for instance, in discussing vitality, Booth observes, "Sustained critical vitality depends on the vitality of many individual critics with a sense of common enterprise. There are, of course, historical mo-

ments of accidental bustle, when the sounds of shooting in every direction give an illusion of vigor. . . . There may even be moments when the best activity would be a 'weeding out' or a 'winnowing'—or even a 'last judgment.' But such moments, if and when they come, depend on the earlier propagations and peaceful inheritances. Unless someone has heard the message, 'go forth, multiply, and replenish the earth,' there will be no weeds to pull, no critical error to be purged, no father to be killed" (*Critical Understanding*, p. 222).

48. I am referring here to what Aristotle called *phronesis*, or "practical wisdom," which combines general principles with perception in a particular situation. See Aristotle, *Nicomachean Ethics*, trans. W. D. Ross, The Great Books (Chicago: University of Chicago Press, 1952), especially 1140a. 32–35. Gadamer in *Truth and Method*, pp. 278–89, retrieves Aristotle's notion of phronesis to develop the dialectical structure of understanding. *Phronesis*, for both Gadamer and Aristotle, depends upon the intersubjectivity of a community.

49. Dietrich Bonhoeffer, *The Cost of Discipleship*, trans. R. H. Fuller (New York: Macmillan, 1958). The best contemporary interpretation of love in the Christian theology is Daniel Day Williams, *The Spirit and the Forms of Love* (New York: Harper & Row, 1968).

Chapter 4: Proclamation as the Word for the World

Epigraphs: Bell Hooks, *Feminist Theory: From Margin to Center* (Boston: South End Press, 1984), p. ix. Hooks is speaking directly about the experience of being on the margin as a black woman and refers to white women as in the center. I do not think Hooks fully understands the complicity of monotheistic ordering in patriarchy; the very ordering of center and margin is constituted in relation to the nature of women as taboo in regard to the religious-political center. On the other hand, Hooks's critique of white women as having a relation to the center that blacks do not have is important.

Margaret Atwood, "Marrying the Hangman," *Selected Poems II: Poems Selected and New 1976–1986* (Boston: Houghton Mifflin, 1987), p. 19; Ursula K. Le Guin, "She Unnames Them," *The New Yorker*, January 21, 1985, p. 27, quoted in Sandra M. Gilbert and Susan Gubar, *No Man's Land: The Place of the Woman Writer in the Twentieth Century*, vol. 1, "The War of Words" (New Haven, CT: Yale University Press, 1988), p. 227.

1. See Gordon Kaufman, *Theology for a Nuclear Age* (Philadelphia: Westminster Press, 1985).

2. See *The Holocaust as Event of Interruption*, ed. Elisabeth Schüssler Fiorenza and David Tracy, *Concilium* 175 (1984).

3. See Lamb, *Solidarity with Victims;* Terrence Des Pres, *The Survivor: An Anatomy of Life in the Death Camps* (London: Oxford University Press, 1976); Elaine Scarry, *The Body in Pain: The Making and Unmaking of the World* (New York: Oxford University Press, 1985); and Justus George Lawler, "Politics and the American Language," in *College English*, National Council of Teachers of English (April 1974): 750–55.

4. Kristeva, "The Pain of Sorrow in the Modern World: The Works of Marguerite Duras," pp. 140–51.

5. Metz, *Emergent Church*, p. 23.

6. Gustavo Gutiérrez, "The Irruption of the Poor in Latin America and the Christian Communities," in *The Challenge of Basic Christian Communities: Papers from the International Ecumenical Congress of Theology*, ed. Sergio Torres and John Eagleson (Maryknoll, NY: Orbis, 1981), p. 92.

7. I do not want to suggest my reading as the only one, or even the only feminist reading. My reading, to use the terms of Charles Taylor in reference to Hegel, is that of an interpretive dialectics, not that of a strict dialectics. This reading attempts to name the order that is implicit in both the psychic destructiveness and in the systematic distortions of modernity. It is not, however, a "cause" or "effect," but, descriptively speaking, the order of things. In this way my project attempts archaeological and genealogical practices similar to those of Michel Foucault in *The Archaeology of Knowledge*, trans. A. M. Sheridan Smith (New York: Pantheon, 1972), and *The Order of Things: An Archaeology of the Human Sciences* (New York: Vintage/Random House, 1973). For a good account of Foucault's interpretive analytics, see Hubert L. Dreyfus and Paul Rabinow, *Michel Foucault: Beyond Structuralism and Hermeneutics*, with afterword by Michel Foucault (Chicago: University of Chicago Press, 1982).

8. Weedon, *Feminist Practice and Poststructuralist Theory*, pp. 137–75.

9. Augustine, *Confessions*, trans. John K. Ryan (Garden City, NY: Doubleday, 1960), 1.8.

10. Foucault, *The Order of Things*. See also Dallymar, "After Babel: "Competing Conceptions of Language," in *Language and Politics*, pp. 1–27; and Tracy, "Radical Plurality: The Question of Language," in *Plurality and Ambiguity*, pp. 47–65.

11. In the not-so-distant past, this assumption has created some extreme problems for theology by way of verification and falsification; see *The Logic of God: Theology and Verification*, ed. Malcom L. Diamond and Thomas V. Litzenburg, Jr. (Indianapolis, IN: Bobbs-Merrill, 1975).

12. Many contemporary authors are quick to point out the necessity of some notion of a decentered subject, see for instance Brown, *Society as Text*. Foucault so decenters the subject that he suggests the disappearance of the subject, or more accurately, the disappearance of the discourse of the subject, in *The Order of Things*. But feminists must move with great caution toward ridding their works of the subject all together, lest woman's power to speak and to write her life be erased through a declaration that now, just as women get to speak their subjectivity in the public, there will no longer be subjects.

13. David S. Pacini, *The Cunning of Modern Religious Thought* (Philadelphia: Fortress Press, 1987), pp. 103–55; see also Christopher Lasch, *The Culture of Narcissism: American Life in an Age of Diminishing Expectations* (New York: Norton, 1978); Paul Zweig, *The Heresy of Self-Love: A Study of Subversive Individualism* (Princeton, NJ: Princeton University Press, 1968).

14. C. B. Macpherson, *The Political Theory of Possesive Individualism: Hobbes to Locke* (Oxford: Oxford University Press, 1962); idem, "Natural Rights in Hobbes and Locke," in *Democratic Theory: Essays in Retrieval* (Oxford: Clarendon Press, 1973), pp. 224–50; Roberto M. Unger, *Law in Modern Society: Toward a Criticism of Social Theory* (New York: Free Press, 1976); Pacini, *The Cunning of Modern*

Religious Thought, pp. 19–37; Zillah Eisenstein, *The Radical Future of Liberal Feminism*, pp. 33–88.

15. Hobbes explains the right of nature, "the liberty each man hath, to use his own power, as he will himself, for the preservation of his own nature; that is to say, of his own life; and consequently, of doing any thing, which in his own judgment, and reason, he shall conceive to be the aptest means thereunto" (*Leviathan*, ed. Macpherson [Penguin, 1982], chap. 14, pp. 189–90).

16. Macpherson, *The Political Theory of Possessive Individualism*, p. 264.

17. Burke, "Prologue in Heaven," in *The Rhetoric of Religion*, pp. 273–316. TL. (The Lord) frequently says to S. (Satan), "But it's more complicated than that" in their discussion concerning language, man *(sic)*, and Word.

18. Julia Kristeva, "Women's Time," in *The Kristeva Reader*, ed. Toril Moi, pp. 193–95.

19. Moi observes in relation to this problem in literary theory: "The central paradox of Anglo-American feminist criticism is thus that despite its often strong, explicit political engagement, it is *in the end* not quite political enough; not in the sense that it fails to go *far* enough along the political spectrum, but in the sense that its radical analysis of sexual politics still remains entangled with depoliticizing theoretical paradigms. There is nothing surprising in all this: all forms of radical thought inevitably remain mortgaged to the very historical categories they seek to transcend. But our understanding of this historically necessary paradox should not lead us complacently to perpetuate patriarchal practices" (*Sexual/Textual Politics*, pp. 87–88).

20. For this argument I am indebted to Zillah Eisenstein's *The Radical Future of Liberal Feminism*. Eisenstein's statement of her thesis is as follows: "The argument put forward here is that all feminism is liberal at its root in that the universal feminist claim that woman is an independent being (from man) is premised on the eighteenth-century liberal conception of the independent and autonomous self. All feminism is also radically feminist in that woman's identity as a sexual class underlies this claim. What this book argues is that both the history and the present formulation of liberal feminism is more complicated than the usual and perfunctory description it elicits" (p. 4).

21. For an account of the public/private ordering that has pervaded Western culture see, Jean Bethke Elshtain, *Public Man, Private Woman: Women in Social and Political Thought* (Princeton, NJ: Princeton University Press, 1981), especially pp. 100–97.

22. Moi, *Sexual/Textual Politics*, pp. 87–88. See also Weedon, *Feminist Practice and Poststructuralist Theory*, pp. 75–85. Feminist poets have been making this point for some time; see, for instance, Frank Davey, *Margaret Atwood: A Feminist Poetics* (Vancouver: Talonbooks, 1984).

23. For examples of "radical feminists" not locating themselves within the Christian tradition, see Starhawk, *Dreaming the Dark: Magic, Sex, and Politics* (Boston: Beacon Press, 1982); idem, *The Spiral Dance: A Rebirth of the Ancient Religion of the Great Goddess* (San Francisco: Harper & Row, 1979); Daly, *Gyn-Ecology* and *Pure Lust*.

24. Kristeva, "About Chinese Women," pp. 145–52.

25. I am indebted to the work of Sallie McFague in *Models of God,* as well as in *Metaphorical Theology: Models of God in Religious Language* (Philadelphia: Fortress Press, 1985). For some time now, McFague has been raising the issues that I am treating. My treatment uses the resources of rhetoric, pragmatism, and poststructuralism in relation to hermeneutical philosophy while McFague's work relies primarily on hermeneutical philosophy.

26. There are, of course, many resources examining metaphor. See, for instance, Paul Ricoeur, *The Rule of Metaphor* (Toronto: University of Toronto Press, 1977); Mary Gerhart and Allan Russell, *Metaphoric Process: The Creation of Scientific and Religious Understanding* (Fort Worth: Texas Christian University Press, 1984); Colin Turbayne, *The Myth of Metaphor* (New Haven, CT: Yale University Press, 1962); and Sheldon Sacks, *On Metaphor* (Chicago: University of Chicago Press, 1978).

27. I am indebted to Millie Feske, Patty Griffith, and Pamela Johnson for many discussions on this point.

28. This, it seems to me, is the very important contribution made by French feminists, especially Helene Cixous, Luce Irigaray, and Julia Kristeva.

29. Kristeva, "About Chinese Women," pp. 144–45.

30. The argument, whether made with religious or scientific warrants, usually connects the submission or domination of women to the need to keep the family intact. For an excellent account of the relationship of women and the family in the United States, see Carl N. Degler, *At Odds: Women and the Family in America from the Revolution to the Present* (New York: Oxford University Press, 1980).

31. Eleanor Flexner, *Century of Struggle: The Woman's Rights Movement in the United States* (Cambridge: Belknap/Harvard University Press, 1975); William O'Neil, *Everyone Was Brave: A History of Feminism in America* (New York: New York Times Book Co., 1971); Olivia Coolridge, *Women's Rights: The Suffrage Movement in America, 1848–1929* (New York: Dutton, 1966); Aileen Kraditor, *The Ideas of the Woman Suffrage Movement 1890–1920* (New York: Columbia University Press, 1965); *Up from the Pedestal: Selected Writings in the History of American Feminism,* ed. Aileen Kraditor (New York: New York Times Book Co., 1975); and Rothman, *Woman's Proper Place.*

32. Rothman, *Woman's Proper Place,* pp. 14–60. This applies to white middle-class women, and not to poor black and white women who did not have sufficient financial resources to procure the trappings and tools of middle-class existence.

33. Burke, *A Grammar of Motives,* p. 24.

34. I am indebted to Elizabeth Fox-Genovese for discussions on the writing of history and the complexity of women's experience.

35. A poststructuralist approach, as I have attempted to employ in this book, addresses the pleasure and pain of women's experience as well as the complicity of women with their own oppression.

36. I am indebted to Mary Pellauer's excellent Ph.D. dissertation, "The Religious Social Thought of Three U.S. Women Suffrage Leaders: Towards a Tradition of Feminist Theology," The Divinity School, University of Chicago, 1980.

37. Mud Flower Collective, *God's Fierce Whimsy: Christian Feminism and Theological Education* (New York: Pilgrim Press, 1985), p. 65.

38. Betty Friedan, *The Feminine Mystique* (New York: Dell, 1964).

39. Kristeva, "Women's Time," pp. 190–93; see also idem, *Tales of Love*, pp. 234–63.

40. McFague, "God as Mother," in *Models of God*, pp. 97–123; see also Eleanor McLaughlin, " 'Christ My Mother': Feminine Naming and Metaphor in Medieval Spirituality," *St. Luke's Journal of Theology* 18 (1975): 356–86, and Caroline Walker Bynum, *Jesus as Mother: Studies in the Spirituality of the High Middle Ages* (Berkeley and Los Angeles: University of California Press, 1982).

41. A popular biographer of Luther explains his terror at his first mass in the following manner, "Utterly limp, he came from the altar to the table where his father and the guests would make merry with the brothers. After shuddering at the unapproachableness of the heavenly Father he now craved some word of assurance from the earthly father. How his heart would be warmed to hear from the lips of old Hans that his resentment had entirely passed, and that he was now cordially in accord with his son's decision!" (Roland H. Bainton, *Here I Stand: A Life of Martin Luther* [New York: Mentor, 1950], p. 30).

42. Ruether, *Sexism and God-Talk*, pp. 85–92, and McFague, *Models of God*, pp. 59–87.

43. I do not want to suggest that a "total revolution" can come through a change in language, but I do want to suggest that language and discourse must be transformed to allow for multiplicity and otherness.

44. Kristeva characterizes the third generation of feminism as one which rejects the dichotomy of male and female as metaphysical: "In this third attitude, which I strongly advocate—which I imagine?—the very dichotomy man/woman as an opposition between two rival entities may be understood as belonging to *metaphysics*. What can 'identity', even 'sexual identity', mean in a new theoretical and scientific space where the very notion of identity is challenged? I am not simply suggesting a very hypothetical bisexuality which, even if it existed, would only, in fact, be the aspiration towards the totality of one of the sexes and thus an effacing of difference. What I mean is, first of all, the demassification of the problematic of *difference*, which would imply, in a first phase, an apparent de-dramatization of the 'fight to the death' between rival groups and thus between the sexes" ("Women's Time," p. 209).

45. Many feminists are opposed to any universal claims. It is important, however, to be aware that universal claims are not necessarily transcendental claims, and that universal claims can have a kind of pragmatic status instead. See Chopp, "Feminism's Theological Pragmatics: A Social Naturalism of Women's Experience," pp. 239–56.

·INDEX OF NAMES·

·INDEX OF SUBJECTS·